UNDERSTANDING BIBLE TEACHING

The New Man

J I Packer MA, D.Phil

Scripture Union

47 Marylebone Lane London W1 6AX

Wm. B. Eerdmans

225 Jefferson Avenue, Grand Rapids, Michigan

© 1974 Scripture Union
First published 1974
First published in this form 1978

ISBN 0 85421 704 5 (Scripture Union)
ISBN 0 8028 1768 X (Wm. B. Eerdmans)

Printed in Great Britain at the Benham Press
by William Clowes & Sons Limited, Colchester and Beccles

General Introduction

There are many commentaries on the Biblical text and there are many systematic studies of Christian doctrine, but these studies are unique in that they comment on selected passages relating to the major teachings of the Bible. The comments are designed to bring out the doctrinal implications rather than to be a detailed verse by verse exposition, but writers have always attempted to work on the basis of sound exegetical principles. They have also aimed to write with a certain devotional warmth, and to demonstrate the contemporary relevance of the teaching.

These studies were originally designed as a daily Bible reading aid and formed part of Scripture Union's Bible Characters and Doctrines series. They can, of course, still be used in this way but experience has shown that they have a much wider use. They have a continued usefulness as a summary and exposition of Biblical teaching arranged thematically, and will serve as a guide to the major passages relating to a particular doctrine.

Writers have normally based their notes on the RSV text but readers will probably find that most modern versions are equally suitable. Many, too, have found them to be an excellent basis for group Bible study. Here the questions and themes for further study and discussion will prove particularly useful—although many individuals will also find them stimulating and refreshing.

ONE

Regeneration

1 : A New Heart
Deuteronomy 30.1–10; Jeremiah 31.31–34; Ezekiel 36.25–27

Scripture views sin as a racial fact, the essence of which is that *man plays God* (see Gen. 3.5f.). Sin estranges us from our Maker, evoking His wrath against our disobedience and destroying our power to heed His word (cf. Rom. 8.6–8; 1 Cor. 2.14). God, however, has taken action. By sending His Son into the world to be the propitiation for our sins (1 John 4.10) He has opened the door to pardon, reconciliation, and restored fellowship. Now by sending His Spirit into our hearts He restores responsiveness, so that we actually pass through this door by faith in Christ (cf. John 6.44f.; 10.25–28). Titus 3.5 calls this inner renewing *regeneration*.

Today's three passages speak of God restoring His people from captivity, which is His 'curse' (Deut. 30.1) on them for breaking His covenant (29.25ff.). All three declare that in faithfulness to His covenant purpose and love for His covenant people God will bring them back to their land and their Lord. Circumcision signified God's covenant commitment to Israel, and His covenant claim upon them; hence, when Deut. 30.6 (cf. v. 8) speaks of God as circumcising Israelite hearts so that they love Him wholly, the meaning is that God will cause covenant communion between Him and them to be fully realized and enjoyed. This is exactly what God predicts through Jeremiah: a day when He will renew covenant fellowship between Himself and Israel, not by ceasing to be their 'husband', but by deepening His work of grace—that is, by so changing their hearts that all will obey Him and know Him and taste His pardoning love. The promise concluding v. 33 is the 'slogan' of God's covenant throughout the Bible and at every stage of God's plan (see Gen. 17.7f.; Exod. 6.7; Zech. 8.8; 2 Cor. 6.16; Rev. 21.3). It means that all God is and has is for His people (Rom. 8.31); and all they are and have must be for Him. The fulfilment of Jeremiah's prophecy through Christ is announced in Heb. 8.6–13 and 10.11–18. Ezekiel's prediction echoes Jeremiah's, adding (1) that God

5

works this inner renewal by His Spirit and (2) that His renewing
of their hearts is a purging from defilement. The thought here is
that sin has made us inwardly dirty, and we need cleansing (25,
cf. Psa. 51.7).

Thus God works regeneration in His almighty love, renewing
the heart (not the physical organ, but the inner man, the real
deep down you and me). In this way a life of faith and godliness
becomes natural, whereas before it was impossible. So human
nature *can* be changed!—praise God!

2 : You must be Born Again

John 3.1–15

Nicodemus came to Jesus as spokesman for the Pharisaic theological circle in Jerusalem (the 'we' of v. 2 and the plural 'you'
of vs. 7, 11f.), apparently to invite the young country rabbi into
the fellowship of this learned society—in other words, to patron-
ize Jesus. But Jesus would not relate to him on that basis. The
abruptness of v. 3 as a response to the politeness of v. 2 reflects,
not rudeness, but a radical discernment of need. Without new
birth, says Jesus, none can see or enter the Kingdom of God. In
Jesus' preaching, the Kingdom appears as a complex of relationships whereby those who live under His rule enjoy God's forgiveness and fatherly care. The Pharisees were looking for God's
Kingdom; Jesus is telling Nicodemus that the Kingdom already
exists, but those not born again can neither detect its presence
nor share its life.

'New birth' is one of Jesus' 'earthly things' (12), i.e. His
parables. (Parable means 'comparison'; metaphors as well as
stories are parables.) The point of the parable is that regeneration
is a completely new beginning. Nicodemus is at first bewildered
through taking the parable literally (4), so Jesus explains that the
'birth' He means is 'of water and the Spirit' (5). His chiding of
Nicodemus, 'a teacher of Israel', for not understanding this (10)
implies that the new birth should be familiar to one who taught
the Old Testament. This makes it natural to refer 'water and the
Spirit', not to Christian baptism, or John's baptism, plus Pentecost (how could Jesus have expected Nicodemus to grasp a
reference to that?), but to the two-sided work of inner renewal
foretold in Ezek. 36.25–27. Jesus pictures this renewal to Nico-

6

demus as a fresh birth, leading to a new Spirit-led life incomprehensible to those outside (8).

Note Jesus' progress of thought. Verses 3–8 say: Would you (i.e. you Pharisaic theologians, you self-appointed authorities on spiritual matters) see and enter the Kingdom of God? Then you must be born again. Verses 9–11 say: Would you be born again? Then you must receive our witness (i.e., Mine, and that of My disciples who already know the new birth and the life of the Kingdom first-hand). Verses 14f. say: Will you receive My witness? Then I tell you to put your faith in the heaven-sent Son of Man who, like the brazen serpent in Num. 21.9, is to be 'lifted up' as a means of life. When Jesus said 'lifted up' He was thinking forward to His crucifixion and exaltation (cf. 8.28; 12.32), though Nicodemus could only have understood 'lifted up' in the sense of being displayed as an object of attention. John 7.50 and 19.39 indicate, however, that light dawned for Nicodemus and he became a disciple.

3 : New Birth Shows Itself

John 1.9–13; 1 John 3.1–10

Without new birth God's approach draws no response from man. The first passage shows this. Taken from the prologue of John's Gospel, it tells us that the Word who came into the world by incarnation was already the source of the light of *general revelation*—inklings of God, His law, and His judgement—which everyone receives, willy-nilly. But we know from Paul that this light is regularly turned into darkness by closing 'the eyes of the heart' (Eph. 1.18) and giving oneself up to fantasies of various kinds (see Rom. 1.19–28). Verses 4f. of John's prologue point to this: the light of general revelation shines in darkness, and if the darkness could *suppress* it and *put it out* (the Greek word means this), it would.

Distinct from *general* revelation is *special* revelation of God's saving grace, which comes through knowledge of the Word incarnate. Verse 9 says that He who already gives general revelation came to be the medium of special revelation too. But man's reaction was the same. His own world, which He made, and His own people, the Jews, rejected Him. Once more the darkness sought to put out the light.

But some responded (12), and to these He gave the right

7

(better, *privilege*) of becoming God's sons—objects, that is, of God's fatherly care (cf. **20.**17) and heirs of His glory (cf. **17.**22; Rom. **8.**17). How was it that they responded? Through being born of God, by a supernatural process distinct from natural birth (13: 'blood' signifies human parentage). Adoption is through faith; faith is through regeneration.

The second passage also moves from adoption (1–3) to the new birth which underlies it (9), and centres on the point that new birth necessarily produces a moral change, because God's 'seed' ('nature', RSV) remains in the regenerate. A reborn man does righteousness, i.e. God's revealed will (7, 10), and declines lawlessness, i.e. sin (4), just as Jesus did (5). The present tenses of vs. 6, 7, 8, 9, 10 have habitual rather than categorical force, as is common in Greek; the verbs in v. 9 should be translated 'commits sin habitually', 'cannot sin habitually'. Chapter **1.**8–10 shows that John does not mean 'never sins'! John insists, however, that where there are no signs of the new life of righteousness (imitation of Christ, vs. 5–7; love of Christians, v. 10) there is no regeneration either, but a person is still the devil's child (10).

4 : Imperishable Seed—Imperishable Hope

1 Peter 1.3–5; 1.22–2.3

The 'living hope' of Christians (so called because it is vivid, and gives energy, and brings life eternal; cf. 'living word', v. 23) is the expectation of risen life with Christ at His 'revelation', i.e. His appearing (7). God's promise is of fellowship with their beloved Saviour (8) in His glory, making their salvation from sin and evil complete (4, 9, 10; 2.2). The adjectives 'imperishable, undefiled, unfading' (4) emphasize that this inheritance belongs to the order of heavenly things that abide, in contrast to the tainted and transient wealth of this world (cf. 1 Cor. **7.**31; Matt. **6.**19–21). Jesus's own resurrection is that on which this hope depends (3); the Christian's new birth, bringing him to faith in Christ (5, 8), is the means whereby it becomes his (3); and the protecting power of God is the guarantee that he will finally attain what he hopes for (5). These facts establish the joyful forward-looking mood that should mark all Christian living.

Chapter **1.**22–2.3, which should be read as a single paragraph, has an ethical thrust. First Peter insists that those who share this hope should love their brothers and fellow heirs in God's family (cf. 3.7f.) with complete sincerity and with all their might (22). Peter's language is searching and challenging: do we love other Christians like that? Then he tells them to renounce the various forms of crooked living (2.1), and to long for 'pure spiritual milk' to make them grow into what they hope to be (2). The 'milk' is surely basic Christian teaching, given by God through the apostles and now found in the Bible (cf. 1 Cor. 3.2; Heb. 5.12f.). New-born babies crave intensely for their milk, as their crying shows; Christians should desire God's instruction with equal intensity. All Peter's demands here, together with his references to brothers and babies, flow from the thought of the new birth, which appears again in v. 23. 'Imperishable seed' (an image of begetting) declares that God's renewal of us by the Spirit lasts for ever, while the description of the 'everlasting gospel', the outward means which God used to bring us to faith, as 'abiding' assures us that the promises of salvation will never prove false.

5 : Risen with Christ

Ephesians 2.1–10

Apart from Titus 3.5, Paul does not speak of regeneration; his way of expressing the thought of new birth is to speak of *new creation* (10; 4.24; 2 Cor. 5.17) whereby the spiritually dead are made alive with Christ (1–7; Col. 2.13f.; Rom. 6.3–11).

Here, being *dead* (1, 5) signifies three things: (*i*) unresponsiveness to God (corpses do not answer when you address them); (*ii*) separation from God's fellowship, which is that 'life' for which we were made (2.12; 4.18, cf. John 17.3; Psa. 36.9); (*iii*) exposure to God's wrath (3)—that is, His present hostility and judgement to come (cf. 5.6). Those who are thus *dead* follow a course of life dictated by the world, the devil and the flesh, a life of disobedience to God (2f.). The Bible has a rich store of picture-words for this disobedience: 'trespasses' in Greek signifies false steps, blundering off the path God set us to walk on, and 'sins' is a picture of repeatedly missing the targets God set us to aim at. Note Paul's insistence in v. 3 that there is something guilty and twisted, self-deifying and anti-God, about all the 'drives' of our fallen nature, desires of the mind—'the lust of the eyes (coveting) and the pride of life' (1 John 2.16)—as well as desires seated in the body.

9

Concerning God's quickening of the spiritually dead, so saving them (5, 8), note:

1. It springs from *love, mercy, grace* and *kindness* so completely without parallel as to be largely beyond our thought. Paul piles up words speaking of the *wealth* and *greatness* of this love (4, 7f., cf. 1.5–8), only to confess finally that it is *immeasurable* and passes knowledge (7; 3.18f.).

2. It takes place *in Christ*, i.e. through the execution of God's eternal plan to make union with His incarnate Son the means of our salvation (1.3). Jesus Christ is the mediator to us of all God's gifts, including newness of life; 'the last Adam became a life-giving Spirit' (1 Cor. 15.45).

3. It catches us up into God's act of *raising Christ from the dead*. The Church is the extension, not of the incarnation, but of the resurrection. Those raised sit with Christ in the heavenlies (6), i.e. they enjoy a hidden life that puts them always 'on top', since He who is ruling the worlds makes all things work for their good (cf. Rom. 8.28).

4. A course of *God-planned obedience* is its goal (10).

It thus appears that our salvation through faith, first to last, is all God's doing, and in no sense ours (8f.); so all the praise for it must be His.

Questions and themes for study and discussion on Studies 1–5

1. What is the relation between new birth and justification?
2. Who are Nicodemus' modern equivalents?
3. Was the new birth a reality under the old covenant?
4. What are the signs that a person has been born again?
5. List the ingredients which make up the Christian hope.
6. How does Eph. 2.1–10 apply to persons who have been Christians as long as they can remember?

TWO

The Pattern Life

6 : The Ten Commandments

Exodus 20.1–17

Whether the Ten Commandments are as familiar as they used to be, or ought to be, is doubtful; but it is possible to know them by heart and still miss much of their meaning, as did the Pharisees in our Lord's day. Note the following points.

1. God gave the commandments to Israel in His character as Yahweh, their God and Redeemer (2). Loyalty to their Lord, and gratitude for His work of grace, were to be the motive of their obedience. They were given the law, not to show them how to earn God's favour and acceptance (they had that already), but to guide them in living the life that would please Him, and bring them the fullness of His blessing (6, 12).

2. Though nine commandments are stated negatively, thus focusing on the points at which lawlessness starts (always a good way of inculcating moral alertness!), positive principles are implied, thus: give your God total loyalty; in all your dealings with Him, think of Him only as He has revealed Himself, and not in any other terms; always be reverent; use your weekly day of rest to worship your Maker and Redeemer (cf. v. 11 with Deut. 5.15), and to help others (Mark 3.2 ff.); respect and love your fellow men, and seek their welfare; respect the sanctity of marriage-vows and the integrity of the opposite sex; respect property; stay truthful and straight; be content with what God has given you. Law-keeping was always a matter, not just of avoiding irreligious and anti-social actions in public, but of loving service to God (6, Deut. 6.5) and one's neighbour (Lev. 19.18).

3. Though stated in terms of outward action, the commandments touch the heart, calling for right desires and attitudes (cf. Jesus' exposition of the sixth and seventh commandments, Matt. 5.21–30).

The commandments were given as God's covenant requirement of Israel, but the principles embodied in them go back to

11

creation, and what they are pointing to is the shape of the ideal life, not just for Israelites, but for man as such. Law-keeping, which is what God's image and likeness involves (cf. Gen. 1.26; Eph. 4.24), is what human nature was made for, and there is no true human fulfilment, just as there is no true godliness, without it.

For an exposition of the Ten Commandments, questions 99 to 148 of the Westminster Larger Catechism, and *The Ten Commandments*, by Thomas Watson (Banner of Truth), are recommended.

7 : Portrait of a Happy Man

Matthew 5.1–12

The Kingdom of God is the reign of Christ over converted sinners, and the Sermon on the Mount is its charter: a discourse for disciples (1 f.), showing in ideal form how citizens of the Kingdom will live, and how God will bless and use them. Controlling the whole Sermon is the thought that God is the Father, and as such the guardian and rewarder, of Jesus' disciples (9; 6.4, 6, 8–15, 18, 26–32; 7.11). The blessings of the beatitudes should be understood as the Father's ways of enriching His children, now and hereafter. 'The kingdom of heaven' in vs. 3, 10 means the family relationship with God through Christ, together with all that flows from it, and the promises of the other beatitudes are of particular 'kingdom blessings' from our Heavenly Father's store.

The nine beatitudes are a series of promises, and those who qualify for the promised gift are spoken of each time as 'blessed'. The Greek word does not mean 'object of blessing', as the English reader might suppose; it means *happy, fortunate, enjoying an enviable lot*. This is paradoxical, for the qualifications include conscious inner poverty (3), mourning (4), dissatisfaction with one's own state (6), and being an object of hatred and ill-treatment (10 f.). But the principles of life in the Kingdom, according to the Sermon, are grace and faith—the free giving of God 'to enrich the humble poor', and the disciple's trust and confidence in God the giver (cf. the definition of faith in Heb. 11.1). It is what God gives to the disciple, not what he has in himself, that makes his lot happy.

The qualities of the happy man may be summarized thus: his sense of inner poverty (3) comes from knowledge of his sinfulness, his mourning (4) from desire to be rid of it, and his craving for righteousness (6) from a passion to please God. He is meek (5) in that he does not assert himself, and when others exploit, abuse and maltreat him because of his Christian stand (10 f.) he quietly accepts it, as from God, not seeking revenge but continuing gentle and loving towards them (see this in Jesus, Matt. 11.29 and 1 Pet. 2.23; and in Moses, Num. 12.3 and the whole chapter). His mercifulness to those who do not deserve mercy (7), and his passion for peacemaking (9), are aspects of his meekness and of his Christlikeness (cf. Heb. 2.17 f.; Mark 9.50; Eph. 2.14). His purity of heart relates not only to the seventh commandment (27 ff.) but to his single-minded determination to seek and serve God in everything rather than indulge himself (cf. 6.19–24). All these qualities, apart from the sense of sin, are seen supremely in Jesus Himself, and the reward promised in each case shows how God delights in them.

8 : An Example

John 13.1–20

Jesus' washing of His disciples' feet during the Last Supper (4) was an acted parable of spiritual cleansing, and thus a token of redeeming love (1, 7–10). As told there, the episode reveals three aspects of His glory:

1. *Jesus' Divine Knowledge.* As Son of God, He knew He would soon return to His Father to reign (1, 3); as Searcher of hearts (cf. 2.25), He knew which of His chosen disciples were 'clean' (i.e. forgiven and accepted by God) and which one was not 'clean' and would betray Him (10 f., 18 f.). Also, He knew that His road back to the Father led through the ultimate humiliation of the cross, the humiliation which He symbolized here by taking the role of a low-grade menial. There is no support here for the idea, canvassed by some, that the conditions of the incarnation limited Jesus' knowledge.

2. *Jesus' Saving Love.* He loved His own 'to the *end*'—that is, according to John's habit of multiple meaning, to the end of His earthly life and of His redemptive work, and also to the last degree. A Jewish host normally had his guests' feet washed by

13

an underling; Jesus, as host at the Supper, does the job Himself, first taking off His coat to reveal Himself as a true Servant in action (4 f.). A modern equivalent of feet-washing would be shoe-cleaning. The initiative, as always, was with Jesus. Simon Peter disapproved of Jesus thus demeaning Himself and, Simon-like, said so (cf. Matt. 16.22 f.). Jesus' words in v. 8, however, made him change his tune, and instead of refusing to have his feet washed he asked for total immersion! Jesus' reply (10) showed that daily cleansing within an already established relation of acceptance was the particular blessing which the feet-washing signified.

3. *Jesus' Divine Authority*. As Teacher, Lord, and Director of His disciples' lives, He charges them to follow His example of loving service. The particular service which the feet-washing signified was unique (i.e., cleansing from sin), but the spirit of love and care which the action revealed is not to be unique: Christians must reproduce it. It is in the first instance by maintaining an attitude of self-humbling love, rather than by particular outward behaviour-patterns, that Christians are called upon to imitate Christ (cf. Eph. 5.1 f.).

9 : The Greatest Thing

1 Corinthians 13

The Greek word *agape* (love) seems to have been virtually a Christian invention, a new word for a new thing (apart from about twenty occurrences in the Greek version of the O.T., it is almost non-existent before the N.T.). For *agape* draws its meaning directly from the revelation of God in Christ. *Agape* is not a form of natural affection, however intense, but a supernatural fruit of the Spirit (Gal. 5.22). It is a matter of will rather than of feeling (for Christians must love even those whom they dislike: Matt. 5.44–48). It is the basic element in Christlikeness. Christian love is '*Calvary* love'. Paul here hymns love as the greatest thing in the world (cf. v. 13), and the 'still more excellent way' (12.31, cf. 14.1) for those who would find God's best.

1. *The Primacy of Love* (1–3). Tongues, prophetic gifts, theological expertise and miracle-working faith (1 f., cf. 12.9 f.; Mark 11.22 f.), all true gifts of God in the apostolic age, pre-occupied the Corinthians; giving everything away and accepting

martyrdom (cf. Mark **10.**22; Luke **12.**33; Matt. **10.**21 f.) may be required of Christians at any time. Yet love matters so much more than these things that without it they all become worthless, and the loveless Christian, however gifted and active, gains nothing and is nothing (i.e. his works will perish, to his shame and loss: 3.10–15). Paul wants the Corinthians to see that the grace of a loving heart is better than any amount of ability and loveless labour.

2. *The Profile of Love* (4–7). These statements about love make up a portrait of Jesus; from this standpoint the four Gospels are the best commentary on them. Also, they comprehensively correct the bumptious, contentious, suspicious, presumptuous, arrogant, self-assertive, critical, irresponsible spirit because of which Paul had to call the Corinthians carnal, and spiritually babyish (3.1; cf. 1.11. f., 3.3; 4.6 f., 18; **5.**2, 6; **6.**8; **8.**1–3; **9.**3; **10.**6–13; **11.**17–22). Love neither condones others' sins (6) nor is hostile, cynical, or exploiting, but is absorbed in seeking others' good.

3. *The Permanence of Love* (8–13). The greater importance of love appears from the fact that it will last through the life to come, when all occasion for tongues, prophecy and theological instruction will have ceased.

10 : Hope and Holiness

1 Peter 1.13–21

Applied to God (the fundamental usage) the word 'holy' signifies everything about Him that sets Him apart from men; notably, His power and purity. Applied to men, the word signifies, first, the relation of being consecrated to God's service and use, and accepted for it, and secondly, the quality of Godlikeness which one displays in one's living. Holiness of life involves both *worship*, in which God's truth draws us out into responsive praise and prayer, and *obedience*, whereby we fulfil the patterns set for us in God's law (cf. 2.9). These are the ideas expressed in the directive of Lev. **11.**44 f. and (quoting Leviticus) vs. 15 f.: 'you (my people) shall be holy, for I (your God) am holy.'

Verses 13 f. work up to this summons. Verse 13 is a warning against three evils which blight the Christian life. The first is being *slack*—so 'gird up your minds', pull yourselves together—

15

concentrate! The second is being *haphazard*, the way of the drunkard—so 'be sober'—discipline yourself, be purposeful and alert! The third is being *double-minded*, the evil that results from looking too hard at the world's present attractions and not hard enough at the prospects held out to us by God's promises—so 'hope *fully*', *fix* your hope on what is to come. Holy living is powerfully motivated by the hope of glory with Christ (cf. v. 21; 1 John 3.2 f.). To Christians who, like Peter's readers, and like Christians living under hostile regimes today, face hardship and ill-treatment for Christ's sake for the remainder of their stay on earth (cf. 4.12–19), such a hope is supremely stabilizing and encouraging (cf. Rom. 8.24 f.). (RSV's 'exile' in v. 17 is a mistranslation: Peter's point is not that they are for the present barred out of Heaven, but simply that this world is only a temporary place of residence, and not their real home.)

Over and above the power of hope, Peter invokes two more motives for holy living. The first is their sense of privilege (18–21), springing from knowledge of three things: first, the *preciousness* of the blood of Christ which was shed for them; second, the *concern* God has shown for their redemption, designating His Son for this task before ever they existed; third, their *adoption* as God's sons and heirs through the new birth (14, 17). The second motive is their sense of reverence for the God who is related to them as a just Judge as well as a loving Father (17). This filial reverence (not panic and terror) is the meaning of the 'fear' of God (17, cf. Psa. 111.10; Prov. 1.7, 29; Acts 9.31).

11 : In His Steps

1 Peter 2.18–25

Christians today, like slaves in Peter's day (18), are often in jobs and relationships where they are not fairly treated, but are made to suffer wrongfully. Now as then, however, there is support for such sufferers in the gospel—support which will make possible the patient endurance (19) which God requires. 'Mindful of God' (19, RSV) is a poor translation: the Greek means 'for the sake of (i.e. in deference to) a God-informed conscience', and points to the Christian's knowledge that he is called to a life of innocent suffering, after Christ's example (21). 'The heirs of salvation, I know from His word, through much tribulation must follow their Lord' (John Newton, cf. Acts 14.22).

16

This is one of many places in the New Testament where a magnificent statement of doctrine slips in quite incidentally to make an ethical point. Verses 22–25 are a rich though compressed review of God's plan of salvation. Peter dwells on Christ's role as God's suffering servant, in language that echoes Isa. 53. He calls attention to Jesus' total innocence (22), and His patience under provocation and pain (23, cf. Matt. 27.12–14; John 19. 8–11). He then explains that His innocent suffering was actually a work of vicarious sin-bearing (24, cf. v. 21; 3.18); he reminds them that God purposed through this to bring them into a new life, in which they said good-bye to sin and lived henceforth by God's law (24, cf. 4.1 f.); and finally he brings before them the fact that they have already turned from their life of sinful wanderings to the living Christ (God's vindication of Jesus through resurrection and exaltation is assumed, though not mentioned), so that Christ has now become their Shepherd and Overseer—that is, leader and protector (25). 'Overseer' is *episkopos*—'Guardian' in the RSV, 'Bishop' in the AV (KJV)—and the phrase reminds us that the pastoral oversight exercised by Christian ministers must always reflect and subserve the perpetual pastorate of Christ Himself.

What Peter wants his readers to learn from all this is that to follow in the steps of our Saviour through suffering is in fact an honour for us (cf. Phil. 1.29)—just as it is something which delights God and wins His approval. Following Christ's example in the New Testament means two things: loving and serving others (as in John 13.1–20, cf. Study 8) and enduring maltreatment while one does so (as here).

Questions and themes for study and discussion on Studies 6–11

1. What place should the ten commandments take in the modern world?
2. What are the links between faith, hope and love in Christian discipleship?
3. Is law-keeping an adequate description of Christian obedience? If not, what needs to be added?
4. In what ways are Christians called to imitate Christ?
5. Murray McCheyne prayed: 'Lord, make me as holy as it is possible for a saved sinner to be.' What would an answer to this prayer involve?
6. Work out in detail what it means to be humble and meek.

THREE

Identification with Christ

12 : The Way of the Cross

Mark 8.31–38; Galatians 2.20; 6.11–18

In the first passage, having stated and reaffirmed against Peter the necessity of His being rejected and executed (31–33), Jesus declares that anyone who would 'come after' Him (that is, learn what it means to go His way) must do three things. First, he must give up all right to himself (34)—that is, cease bothering about self-preservation (35), self-aggrandizement (36), and self-protection against ridicule (38), and abandon self-assertion as a way of life. This is the condition in which 'the world is crucified to me' (Gal. 6.14). Second, he must take up his cross—that is, settle for a life into which the world's favour and esteem do not enter. Only criminals going to execution—men, that is, from whom the world's favour had been totally withdrawn—carried crosses in those days (cf. John 19.17). This is the condition in which one is 'crucified to the world' (Gal. 6.14). Third, the would-be disciple must 'follow' Jesus in the sense of accepting as leader and guide One who was even then on His way to crucifixion, and who expected to involve His disciples in sufferings corresponding to His own (10.39; Matt. 10.25). This, says Jesus, is the only path that leads to life (35).

In the second passage, having told how he, a Jew, came to see that the law had not brought him righteousness and life (16, 21; 3.21 f.), but only a necessity of death (19), Paul states that his acceptance of Christ, and Christ's cross, as his only means of life with God, had involved accepting the law's death-sentence on him and regarding himself henceforth as having been 'crucified with Christ'. My old life, says Paul, has finished—under judgement; now, by faith in the Christ who died for me—the Christ who now lives for me—I live the new life of self-denial, Christ-centred, Christ-indwelt, and Christ-controlled, and I find it to be life indeed. The two aspects of the Christian's identification with Christ—acceptance of His cross as both the end of one's old life and the pattern of one's new life—are here brought together.

18

In Gal. 6.11–18, the postscript in Paul's own handwriting (11), Paul insists that true Christianity—that is, 'new creation' (15) and the enjoyment of God's peace and mercy (16)—flows from accepting total solidarity with Christ's cross, embracing it as one's path and passport to life, and making it one's only pride and joy (14).

13 : Risen, Freed, and Enslaved

Romans 6

This great chapter teaches that saving union with Christ by faith brings 'newness of life' (4) through incorporation into Christ's own dying and rising. Christ's person, cross and resurrection, although historically located in Palestine in about A.D. 30 are 'trans-historical' realities. The risen Christ 'fills all things' (Eph. 4.10): every believer everywhere in every age touches Him, lives 'in' Him, and is made new by Him. From co-crucifixion and co-resurrection with Christ flow freedom from sin's dominion (6 f., 14, 16–18), a new enslavement to God and to righteousness (18, 22), the hope of bodily resurrection (5, 8–10), and eternal life as God's free gift (23). There follows also an obligation not to let indwelling sin regain mastery at any point (12–19). You need never give in to sinful urges, says Paul (14), and that is something to thank God for (17), since bondage to sin brings only death (21). Paul's theme here is new creation (cf. 2 Cor. 5.17); his point is that those who are 'under grace' (14 f.) must live differently from before, because in Christ they really are different people.

Particular points to note:

1. Verse 1 means 'Shall we carry on under sin's sway as before?' —to which v. 2 replies that since we are different we can't, and should not dream of trying.

2. Baptism-imagery is used in vs. 3 f. because Christian baptism is a sign of initiation (starting a relationship with Christ), termination (ending one's old life), dedication, and renewal.

3. Sin (6, 12, 14, 16, 18, 20, 22) is an anti-God 'drive', or 'twist' of nature, mastering unbelievers and still indwelling Christians (7.17, 20, 23). Sin will remain with us as long as our bodies are 'mortal' and unrenewed (12, cf. 8.23). This, and not any depreciation of physical nature as such, is the point of Paul's references to the body of 'sin' and 'death' (6.6; 7.24).

4. 'Know' (3, 6, 9, 16), 'believe' (8), 'consider' (11) are key words: for the basis of Christian holiness is taking God's word about the inward change He has effected and then living out what He has wrought in (cf. Phil. **2**.12 f.).

5. 'Yield' (13, 16, 19), or 'present', implies consent of will. Paul is calling for a life of repentance and consecration (19, 22, where 'sanctification' means 'consecrated state', cf. **12**.1 f.). He is not here discussing the continuing involuntary shortcomings of the consecrated, which he deals with in Rom. 7.14–25; 8.23; Gal. 5.17.

6. It is through faith's obedience to gospel truth that the inward work of grace replacing sin's rule by God's becomes a reality (**17**).

14 : Holding Fast the Head

Colossians 2.6–19

Verses 6–8 sum up the message of Colossians. Let Jesus Christ be everything to you, says Paul; live (literally 'walk') 'in Him' (6), acknowledging Him as the ground in which you are rooted and the One who builds you up in the Church (cf. v. 19), for whom you should constantly give God thanks (7, cf. 3.17), because of the 'wealth' and 'treasures' He has brought you (1.27; **2**.3). And don't be 'conned' by any supposed 'wisdom' from non-Christian sources, whether ordinary 'worldly wisdom' or derived from the occult, into doing anything else (8)! 'Philosophy' here means heretical theosophy; 'the world', 'human tradition', emanates from human society organized without God and banded against God; on the 'elemental spirits' or 'rudiments', see note on Study 15.

Paul's directive follows from his doctrine of who and what Christ is. In His own right as God's incarnate Son and Image (1.13–15, 19; 2.9), Maker and Master of the universe and Lord of the Church (1.16–18), and also as the complete answer to our spiritual needs (10) through His atonement for our sins (1.20; 2.13 f.), His indwelling in our hearts (1.27), and the new life with God that He brings (13), Christ is and must be pre-eminent (1.18). Paul piles up imagery, sacramental and secular, to high-light Christ's adequacy. In Christ, he says, God has renewed your hearts (inward circumcision and burial in baptism, vs. 11 f.). Having found you spiritually dead, He brought you to life with Christ through faith (risen in baptism and forgiven, vs. 12 f., cf.

20

Eph. 2. 1 ff.). Through the cross He cancelled our death sentence which the broken law demanded (14) and overthrew all the forces of cosmic evil. For those who have eyes to see, Christ's cross, which looked like a humiliating defeat, was actually His march of triumph, in which He led His foes captive, in the manner of a Roman general after a successful campaign (15).

Paul's central point is that nobody needs more than Christ gives. For a Christian to turn to Judaizing ritualism (16 f.), angel-worship (18), and the murky world of 'visions' (18), is not gain, but loss. Christ alone makes the Church (His body) live and grow spiritually. Christians must 'hold fast to the Head' (19), and not seek spiritual enrichment from other sources; it is not there to be had, and to seek it is to lose touch with Christ. Paul is attacking the particular errors of the Colossian theosophists, but modern occultism and superstition fall equally under his apostolic ban.

15 : Christ is our Life

Colossians 2.20–3.15

The deepest reason why Christians must accept identification with Christ as the controlling principle for their lives is that God has actually united them with Christ in His dying and rising. When Christ rose, He ascended to God's 'right hand', i.e. a state of glory and dominion in His Father's immediate presence. When Christians are made alive in Christ, they at once enter into this same realm of spiritual realities, transcending space and time, where they have fellowship with the Father and the Son (cf. 1 John 1.3). Christ is henceforth their 'life' in the sense that all their communion with God flows from Him and relates to Him, and will continue so for ever. This 'life' of theirs is hidden so far as the eye of sense is concerned, just as Christ Himself is; but when Christ is manifested in glory at His coming, Christians will be with Him, and His relation to them as their life will then be plain to see (3 f.).

The presupposition of our enjoying this 'life' is that we 'died' with Christ—that is, finished with the world and its ways (20). Whether we died to 'elemental spirits', i.e. bad angels, the 'world-rulers of this present darkness' (Eph. 6.12)—so RSV—or to the 'rudiments' of the world's wisdom—so AV (KJV)—is disputed, but the point is in either case the same. A clean break with the past has been made (death is the cleanest break imaginable). The 'old man' has been put off and the 'new man' put on (3.9 f.; the image is of changing clothes). What goes on now is a new life entirely, a life which the world does not control. This is the situation into which God has brought all who have received Christ; and now we must live it out.

How are we to do that? First, by recognizing that the world's way of religion (such things as legalism, man-made restrictions, holiness equated with abstinence and austerity) is in truth just one more form of self-indulgence which must be given up (20–23). Second, we must recognize that the world's way of behaviour (self-indulgence in immorality; exploiting others in hostility) must be 'put to death' (3.5–9). By sustained renunciation (9, cf. Gal. 5.24), self-watchfulness, and praying to Christ in the Spirit (cf. Matt. 26.41; Rom. 8.13; Heb. 2.18; 4.15 f.) we are to break the behaviour patterns that were formerly habitual to us (5–7). Third, as those whom God has loved, chosen, forgiven, and renewed to bear the family likeness (10, 12 f.), we must actively 'put on' the Christlike behaviour patterns described in vs. 12–15.

Questions and themes for study and discussion on Studies 12-15

1. 'Yet not I, but Christ lives in me.' Does this mean the obliterating of Paul's personality? If not, why not, and what does it mean?
2. In what ways is it true that God's service is perfect freedom?
3. What are the symptoms of religious self-indulgence, and how can it be cured?
4. Think out in relation to our various earthly passions (cf. Col. 3.5–9; Rom. 6.12) what it means to 'put them to death' (=mortify them).

FOUR

Growth in Grace

16 : Abide in Christ

John 15.1–17

Jesus' parable of Himself as the vine and His disciples as His branches shows how He in person is the Christian's life, just as Paul's figure of Christ as head and Christians as limbs (members) of His body illustrates how He animates disciples for His service (cf. Rom. **12.**4–8; Eph. **4.**7–16). Union and communion between Him and us are in both cases the basic thought. The Old Testament sees Israel as God's vine (Psa. **80.**8–16, cf. Isa. **5.**1–7); in calling Himself the 'true' vine (i.e. the real one, as opposed to that which was typical and imperfect) Jesus implies that He and His 'branches' are God's true Israel.

The parable, stated in vs. 1–8 and commented on in vs. 9–17, teaches that:

1. God the Father has His hand on Christ's disciples. He wants them to 'fruit', i.e. to be Christlike in character, hardworking in God's service, and influential for good and godliness (1 f., 8, 16, cf. Psa. **1.**3; Matt. **13.**8, 23; Rom. **7.**4; Gal. **5.**22 f.; 2 Pet. **1.**8). Therefore He 'prunes' fruitful branches to make them fruit better (2)—that is, He 'cuts them back' through humbling and chastening providences, so improving their quality. Barren branches (professed Christians whose faith, being merely mental and not touching the heart, is in James's sense 'dead': see Jas. **2.**14–17, 26) He cuts off entirely, by adverse providences here or judgement hereafter (2, 6). Thus He tends His vine.

2. The condition of fruitfulness is to abide in Christ (4 f.), as objects of His abiding love (10). 'Abide' means simply 'stay' (4, 6, 7, 9, 10), and the way to *stay* is to *obey* (10). Christ's obedience to His Father (10), in loving those He calls friends up to the point of dying for them (12–15, 17) is the model here: Christ directs us to love in the same way. Humility and self-distrust (5b), sustained attention to Christ's command as we move among men (7), and total reliance on Him for enabling grace, are all involved; we shall not be able to stay steady in Christ without them.

23

3. Those who stay in Christ may pray confidently and successfully, for (*a*) their will and His will coincide (7) and (*b*) they may ask 'in his name' (16)—that is, invoking His authority as the Author of their right to pray, the Authorizer of their particular requests, and indeed the Father's Agent in granting them (cf. 14.14). To enter into this promise of prevailing in prayer, we must seek above all to know Christ's will; the major task in petitionary prayer is getting from the Lord Himself the requests to be made.

17: Knowing and Growing

Ephesians 1.15–23; 3.14–21

In the first passage Paul starts a prayer from which the doctrinal excursion of ch. 2 diverts him. Chapter 3.14–19, following another diversion in vs. 2–13, completes the prayer. Paul asks the Father of the one Saviour and the one family (1.17, cf. v. 3, 3.14 f., cf. 2.17; 4.6) that his readers may *know* the wealth of their salvation (1.18 f.) and the greatness of Christ's love (3.19), and that, through this knowledge they may *grow*, i.e. 'be filled with'—so RSV, but 'be filled up to' would be more accurate—'all the fullness of God' (3.19). The thought is of sharing, and so embodying, and thereby reflecting all the richness of life and all the moral excellences which God's work as Creator and Redeemer in Christ has displayed. As the 'knowing' is a corporate destiny only happening in fellowship 'with all the saints' (1.18), so is the 'growing'. It takes all the saints together to come to 'a mature man'—the RSV's 'mature manhood' blunts the point—'the measure of the stature of the fullness of Christ' (4.13–15). It requires the whole church to be Christ's fullness (1.23); He has more to give, and there is more in Him to be embodied, than any one of us can contain.

The realities which Paul wants Christians to know—that is, to know better than they do at present—make a striking list. First is the *hope* belonging to those whom God has called—the prospect, that is, of being filled up to God's fullness through enjoyment of grace here and glory hereafter (1.18). Second is the rich *inheritance* God gives 'in the saints' (i.e., in their experience, cf. the use of 'in' in Gal. 1.16)—a related thought, focusing on the notion of immeasurable personal wealth (18). Third is the greatness of God's *power* towards believers here and now—power that may be estimated in part from the raising and exalting of Jesus (19–23), and the spiritual resurrection and re-creation which believers have already undergone (2.1–10). In the closing doxology (3.20 f.) Paul adoringly acknowledges that, just as Christ's love is more than we can know fully (3.17–19), so is God's power—but in neither case do the limits of our thought set limits to the reality. Fourth is God's *love* in Jesus Christ, of which we have just spoken—the love revealed in Christ's suffering for worthless wrongdoers and God's consequent quickening of them (cf. 1.6–8; 2.4–7; Rom. 5.6–8; 1 John 4.8–10; 3.1). The supreme need of Christians is still to know these things. But such knowledge is not natural; it comes through enlightenment by the Spirit (1.17 f.; 3.16), knowledge of the indwelling Christ (3.17), and a prior commitment to the life of love (17), and must be sought from God Himself.

18 : Man of One Thing

Philippians 3

Paul wants to enforce his summons to joyful exultation in Christ (1, 3, cf. 4.4) and total distrust of the 'flesh'—meaning here pedigree, privilege (e.g. circumcision) and performance (4–6). So he cites himself as an example (17) of one who had more reason for confidence in the flesh than anyone he ever knew, yet renounced it, and now saw all he once valued and relied on as mere 'dung' (8). The metaphor is coarse and violent, as it would be in a letter or sermon today, but it exactly expresses Paul's thought—worthless and unattractive refuse; 'droppings' to be left behind and forgotten (4–8, 13). All that was 'gain' to Paul, giving him as he thought a head start with God, he now regarded as 'loss', setting him off on the wrong foot and diverting him from Christ; so he had let it all go (8).

How came this mental revolution? Through knowing 'Jesus Christ my Lord' as the bringer of righteousness from God—that is, a right relationship with God (9, cf. Rom. 1.16 f.). This relationship, unattainable by the moral athletics of Pharisaism, is Christ's gift to those who trust Him. Paul was 'blameless' touching the law only by the Pharisees' external standards (6); Christ showed the inadequacy of these standards (Matt. 5.20–48; Mark 2.23–3.6), and condemned the self-righteousness based on them (Luke 18.9-14, cf. Rom. 10.3). Elsewhere, Paul says that before conversion he was, inwardly at least, an active and lost sinner (Rom. 7.7-11).

Knowing Christ brought Paul a new integration and purpose. He became a man of one thing (13), going 'flat out' like a runner in a race to know more of Christ and enter into the dying-to-live experience which is the Christian's road to glory, as it was Christ's own (10 f., cf. 2 Cor. 4.6-12; Heb. 12.1-3). With Christ as his path, prize and Saviour at the end of the day, Paul's life was dominated by the resolve to run for home which certainty of final salvation always imparts (20 f., 12-14, cf. 1.6, 21). (What 'if possible' in v. 11 expresses is not doubt of the outcome, but self-deprecating wonder at it.) So to live, making each particular activity a conscious doing of the one thing at motivational level, and eschewing earthly-mindedness like the plague (18 f.), is a mark of Christian maturity (15).

19 : Practical Holiness

1 Thessalonians 3.11-4.12

'Holiness' (3.13) and 'sanctification' (4.3—and vs. 4, 7 where 'holiness' represents the same Greek word) are from a single root. The former means a state of being set apart for God, the latter the event or process whereby this apartness comes about. Paul speaks of God 'sanctifying' men in two senses, first by taking them into fellowship at conversion (so 1 Cor. 6.11; 1.2) and second by keeping them from entanglement with sin thereafter (so 1 Thess. 5.23). But God's way of keeping us is to empower us to keep ourselves (cf. Phil. 2.12 f.; Jude 21), and so sanctification is presented to us, not only as God's work (cf. 1 Cor. 1.30), but also as our ethical target. So here. From this standpoint, sanctification means breaking with the world's ways to do God's will, and holiness means the condition in which this break has been fully made.

What this passage says about holiness may be put thus:

1. Holiness is *not optional*. Sanctification is God's will for all Christians (4.3). It is a matter of obeying instructions which come with God's call to salvation (4.1 f., 7); it starts with the heart (motive and inward commitment, 3.13) and is then expressed in

26

conduct. Holiness pleases God (1), but unholiness in any form sooner or later calls down His retributive action (6).

2. Holiness entails *avoiding sexual immorality* (**4**.3–8). The right course is to marry 'in holiness and honour' (4), respecting one's partner as a person made in God's image and the marriage relation as God's own ordinance of a lifelong bond. What v. 5 disapproves is not sexual affection as such, but using one's partner to please oneself rather than oneself to please one's partner—which was and is the pagan way in both marriage and more casual relationships. Clandestine adultery and overt wife-swapping are equally condemned by v. 6; in either case, the person whose partner is taken by another is exploited and wronged (cf. David and Uriah, 2 Sam. **11–12**).

3. Holiness involves *loving action towards both Christians and non-Christians* (3.12; **4**.9 f.). Holiness is more than abstaining from all evil (cf. **5**.22); Christian love is the way separation to the Christian God must show itself.

4. Holiness requires *willingness to work*, so as to be independent. Sponging and scrounging have no place in the true life of faith (11 f., cf. 2 Thess. **3**.6–12).

5. Holiness involves *minding one's own business*, and not being a nosey gossip (11). How down-to-earth Paul is!

20 : On to Maturity

Hebrews 5.11–6.3

God made us rational and deals with us rationally; so every stage of Christian advance, from conversion on, is a response to apprehended truth. Where knowledge fails, progress with God is impossible. Chapter **5**.11–14 complains that, after years as believers, these Jewish Christians were neither passing on the truth they knew nor holding it fast themselves (let alone hungering for more, as they should have been); instead, they had regressed to a sort of spiritual infancy in which even elementary things had ceased to be clear and they needed to learn the gospel ABC all over again. Blurred vision regularly results from not facing spiritual challenges squarely, and in this case the challenge to patience under persecution was not being faced (**6**.12; **10**.32–36; **12**.12 f.). In their self-induced infantile state, they could scarcely take the 'solid food' (teaching on Christ's perfect high-

27

priesthood, with its implications of finality and exclusiveness) which the writer had for them, and gives in chs. 7–10.

What they lacked was *maturity* (noun, 6.1; adjective 5.14)— that is, the 'perfection' of the fully-developed, clear-sighted, whole-hogging spiritual all-rounder. The sign of immaturity was that they could not see that the ministry of Christ cancels and excludes the typical religion of the Old Testament, so that by reverting to Judaism, as they thought of doing, they would gain nothing (for they would find no grace there) and would lose everything (for they would incur supreme judgement for supreme sin in rejecting Christ: vs. 4–8). This blindness showed lack of capacity to distinguish good from evil courses—a capacity which requires constant consecrated exercise for its development (14, cf. Eph. 5.15–17; Phil. 1.9 f.). Regressing to spiritual babyhood, they had embraced fantasy and lost touch with spiritual realities. To lead them on to the maturity they lacked and needed, the writer resolves to leave the gospel ABC (which, to his own way of thinking, had been the area of his concern in the earlier chapters) and go on to the more demanding doctrine which, though hard, would do the trick if only they grasped it (6.1–3).

On the ABC (6.1 f.), note: (*i*) 'dead' works are those which bring death because they are evil (cf. 9.14); (*ii*) 'faith toward God' is the theme of chs. 3, 4, 11, 12, cf. especially 11.1, 6; (*iii*) 'washings' is probably a broad reference to the principle that cleansing is a precondition of access to God, taught by Old Testament ceremonial washings (cf. 9.9–14, especially v. 10) and confirmed by the symbolism of Christian baptism (10.22); 'laying on of hands' is probably a sign of welcome into the Christian fellowship, with prayer for spiritual enrichment (cf. Acts 8.15–17).

21 : Confirm your Call

2 Peter 1.1–11

God's calling (3, 10) is the main theme here. Note:

1. Like Paul (cf. Rom. 8.28, 30; Gal. 1.15; Eph. 4.1), Peter views God's calling as not only the sending of an invitation to life through faith, but also a work of divine power (3) eliciting the faith required and so imparting knowledge of Jesus Christ as Saviour (2, 3, 8, cf. 2.20, 3.18). Strictly, it is Christ Himself who

28

calls, not 'to' (as AV [KJV] and RSV) but 'by'—by the impact of His 'glory' and 'excellence'. These nouns epitomise His divine-human perfection displayed in the gospel (cf. John 1.14; Mark 7.37).

2. Response to God's calling, and the knowledge of Christ given with it, is Peter's key thought for understanding the Christian life. One must not be unproductive in relation to this knowledge (8); the unproductive man has lost touch with reality—the reality, that is, of his having been cleansed from sin by divine forgiveness, sealed in baptism, precisely in order that he might stay clean and keep God's commandment (9, cf. 2.20–22). The calling is to escape disintegration through unbridled desire, which is the world's state and fate (4); so the Christian must practise self-control (6). Again, the calling is to partake of the divine nature (4); so the Christian must imitate God by virtue, God-centredness (the heart of godliness) and love (5–7). Further, the calling rests on promise (4); so the Christian must be steadfast (6), focusing on God's faithfulness and holding fast his hope.

3. One's calling, and the divine election underlying it, are to be made sure—confirmed, that is, to oneself (the middle voice of the Greek verb in v. 10 makes this clearer than English can make it). How are they confirmed? By cultivating the qualities listed in vs. 5–7 as the proper companions, indeed fruits, of faith. For these are evidence that one really has been called to share 'all things that pertain to life *and godliness*' (3). Here is the biblical link between conduct and assurance. The passage is a good basis for honest self-scrutiny.

4. 'Supplement' and 'richly provided' (5, 11) are the same Greek word, meaning 'supply unstintingly', 'provide at whatever cost to oneself'. Peter is teaching that if we lay ourselves out to fulfil our calling, making an effort (5) so that its fruits 'abound' (8), God will also lay Himself out to fulfil 'richly 'His promise of final glory—a thrilling thought!

22 : Look Forward, and Grow

2 Peter 3.11–18

Expectation of meeting Christ at His return (whether or not our own death has preceded) dominates the New Testament view of life. Conduct is assessed by asking how it will look on that day when all secrets are disclosed (cf. Luke **12**.1–3; Rom. **2**.1–16; 1 Cor. **3**.10–15; 1 Thess. **5**.23); moral stability is enforced by reminders that faithfulness will then be rewarded (Matt. **24**. 45–51; 1 Cor. **15**.58; Gal. **6**.7). Peter is on this wavelength (11 f.). He has four things to say:

1. *Hold fast the certainty of Christ's coming.* Then as now, some, disillusioned by delay, were sceptical and contemptuous of this hope (3.3 f.). Peter met their criticisms, pointing out that God's time-scale is not ours (8), that God has merciful reasons for delay (9), and that Christ's coming will in any case be unexpected (10, cf. Matt. **24**.43 f.). His positive point is that the coming is a certainty because God has promised it (2, 9, 13, cf. **1**.4). Christians must live in the light of this knowledge (17).

Verses 10–12 have an uncannily modern ring: what Peter describes is exactly like a nuclear explosion.

2. *Live in readiness for Christ's coming.* Those who expect it (12, 14) should get ready for it (11), pursuing holiness, sitting loose to this world's entanglements, and avoiding all that is disruptive among men and blameworthy before God (14). In this, as in cultivating Christlikeness (**1**.5) and seeking assurance (**1**.10), zeal should be shown and effort exerted (14); apathy and half-heartedness will not do.

3. *Understand the delay in Christ's coming.* Peter juxtaposes two startling thoughts: first, that God delays the day out of compassionate patience, so that more may be saved (9, 15); second, that Christians hasten on the day (12, RSV; AV [KJV] rendering 'hasting unto' is wrong) by the quality of their lives. With 'holiness and godliness' (11) may be included prayer (Matt. **6**.10; Rev. **8**.3 f., **22**.20, etc.); both contribute to making the day dawn.

4. *Grow spiritually while awaiting Christ's coming.* Knowledge about Christ, and first-hand experience of His grace, should increase daily. Christians must not stand still (18)!

Note, incidentally, how Peter brackets Paul's letters with 'the other Scriptures' (16)—a most significant attestation.

FIVE

The Word of God and Life in Christ

23 : Teach me Thy Way

Psalm 119.1–16

To our book-conscious age, the first thought which the phrase 'word of God' suggests is of printed scriptures. To the psalmists, however, the phrase signified rather a body of divine instruction ('law', *torah*), written indeed for reference, but for the most part handed down orally; a body of instruction whose very existence was a sign of God's favour. Idols are impotent and dumb, but Israel's God was both saviour and speaker, and Israel was privileged to enjoy both His grace and His teaching (cf. Psa. 147.19 f.). God had declared His will in both senses (purpose and command), and godliness meant precisely living by His word. The grace and power of God's word is a recurring theme in the psalms (cf. 19.7–11), with Psa. 119 (176 verses, all but one mentioning it directly) as its richest statement. The psalmist treasures the word in his heart and memory (11, 16), dwells on it and delights in it (14–16), looks to it to keep him from sin and teach him the way of life (9–12), and longs to practise it fully (5–8). In this there is continuity between Old Testament piety and its Christian counterpart; Christians too have God's word, the two Testaments together, and for them too God's word is the main means of guidance, grace, and growth.

Along with the *fact* of God's word, this passage indicates its *forms*, viewing it from many angles. 'Word' (9, 11, 16) means 'message'; 'law' means instruction, as from a father to his family; 'testimonies' (2, 14), 'statutes' (5, 8, 12, 16), 'judgements' or 'ordinances' (7, 13), 'precepts' (4, 15), 'commandments' (6, 10), are moral imperatives. Reference to the 'blessedness' of those who walk in the law (1 f.), and the pin-pointing of 'seeking God' as the heart of law-keeping (2, 10), are reminders that the word includes promises (cf. v. 49, etc.) and reveals God Himself (cf. v. 18). The word is God's medium of communication and communion with man, in all the many-sidedness of His relationship with us.

31

Finally, these verses show the *fruit* of God's word. It elicits desire for obedience (5), prayer for instruction (12), and wholehearted seeking of God (2, 10); it cleanses the way, diverting us from what defiles (9); it moves us to speak for God (13) and find our joy in Him (14, 16). Thus through the word of God the work of God goes on in human lives.

24 : The Blessedness of the Righteous

Psalm 1

Psalm 1 is the keynote psalm, setting the tone and focusing the outlook of the whole psalter. It is a meditation showing the profile of the godly man ('the righteous', 5 f.), comparing him with the ungodly, and implicitly urging us to identify with him. The *blessedness* of the righteous—that is, their happiness under God's blessing—is the theme. Nothing said here is affected by the transition from Old to New Testament conditions; these spiritual realities are unchanging.

First, the *way* of the righteous (1 f.) is contrasted with that of his opposite number (6). The godly eschew the thoughts and plans, interests and attitudes of those who scoff at godliness and defy God (1). Instead, they delight in God's law. Why? Because they delight in God Himself, of whom the law testifies and from whom it derives. 'Law' here means God's instruction as a whole, including along with ethical directives covenant promises, and it is knowledge of the grace of these promises that brings the delight (2). D. L. Moody was right to say that either the Bible will keep you from sin or sin will keep you from the Bible; since God's law condemns sin, one cannot delight in both at the same time. Biblical thinking about morality, here as everywhere, resolves into a direct antithesis between God's law and sin.

The *fruit* of the righteous (3) is a matter of Godlikeness in conduct, influence for good, and positive contribution to others' welfare. In this sense, the ungodly are conspicuously unfruitful; sin being a disintegrative force, its servants bring themselves and the world only misery. The godly man's fruit is consistent and regular, like that of a tree rooted by a river and fed by the water in the ground. The picture is of God supplying through his meditation on the word strength for all good works (cf. 2 Tim. 3.16 f.). His universal prospering is inward; since he tries to do

32

everything for God's praise, according to the word, he is enriched by the inner contentment of a good conscience, even when his endeavours are outwardly frustrated and abortive.

His *stability* (5 f.) is due not only to his inner integration, but to the fact that God knows his way, i.e. accepts and watches over him. In the final judgement he will 'stand', i.e. be confirmed in God's favour, while the ungodly, whose way is unacceptable, will fall (6). Scripture regularly evaluates ways of life by noting how they will fare at the judgement.

25 : If You Continue ...

Matthew 7.24-27; John 8.30-37

Today, as when Jesus was on earth, His message remains the prime means of both grace and judgement, according to whether it is embraced or not. The burden of the 'words' (Matt. 7.24) which formed His 'word' (John 8.31) was the way of discipleship: how to live in the Kingdom of God under the King. After Pentecost, the apostles filled in much of the doctrine of grace by their elaboration of what the cross and resurrection had achieved, but they added little to the account of the life of grace, the 'Kingdom ethics', which Jesus had taught.

Central to this 'word' was Jesus' absolute and unqualified demand to be acknowledged as teacher, saviour and master (prophet, priest and king). This is faith, as Jesus taught it. In urging His hearers to 'do' and 'continue in' His word, He was calling them to the obedience of faith. Response to His call would be the mark of a 'wise' person, that is (as always in the Bible), a prudent realist who faces facts, thinks of the future, and picks out under God's guidance the rewarding, as distinct from the ruinous, way to live (Matt. 7.24 f.).

Continuance in Jesus' word is the only sure sign of being in grace. This is Jesus' point in the second passage. Certain Jews had 'believed on' Him in the superficial and inconclusive sense of being impressed by Him without yet knowing enough about Him to see what true commitment and discipleship were all about. Such 'belief'—half-way to faith, but equally half-way from it, and not always issuing in it—appears in John 2.23, and in the stony-ground hearers in the parable of the sower and the soils (see Matt. 13.5 f., 20 f.). Here, Jesus' very invitation to continue

33

gave offence: 'belief' evaporated and they wished Him dead (37)
So fickle can religious people be when faced with their real
spiritual need! Was it this side of Jesus' teaching that set Judas
against Him?

Unreality (because they were a Roman-occupied nation) and
conceit on account of their religious privileges shine out in the
Jews' words in v. 33. Jesus was offering them the freedom from
sin's dominion which Paul celebrates in Rom. 6. But they
resisted His word, turned the offer down, and thus established
their character as foolish men, heading for spiritual judgement
and disaster (35; Matt. 7.26 f.).

26 : Word of Grace and Power

Acts 2.41, 42; 20.29–32; Colossians 3.16, 17

'Grace enters by the understanding.' So said Thomas Aquinas
and the Puritans, and they were right. God deals with us, not as
sticks and stones or robots, to be moved by physical force, but
as thinking persons; and as such He leads us into maturity and
wisdom by stimulating our minds. More than that is involved,
no doubt, but not less. Hence God's Word, His biblically-
recorded message, read, preached, and understood, is the prime
means of grace. It instructs and challenges us, and is able to
change us, because the Spirit makes us attend to it. Through
taking in God's message, chewing it over and digesting it—the
process which Scripture calls *meditation*—faith grows and lives
are transformed.

This message is the word of the *apostles*, for they preached it
(Acts 2.41); it is the word of God's *grace*, for it declares His
redeeming love (20.32); and it is the word of *Christ*, who is both
its source and its theme (Col. 3.16).

In the first passage the Word is the basis of *fellowship*. Accepting the apostolic message opened the door to a common life in
which other 'means of grace' were shared, namely, the Lord's
Supper and the prayers. Without prior acceptance of apostolic
truth, however, such sharing would have been a hollow sham.
For there is only one Christ, the Christ of apostolic teaching,
and the only true basis for the Church's corporate life is a shared
faith in Him, based on shared beliefs about Him. This, be it said,
still applies.

34

In the second passage the Word is a means of *edifying*, i.e. upbuilding. Having warned the Ephesian pastors of doctrinal corruptions to come (30), Paul 'passed them over' (the word means this) to God, who by the word of His grace could build Christians up and bring them to glory despite everything. 'Sanctified' here belongs to the same realm of ideas as 'saints', and refers to God's act of setting men apart for Himself through repentance and regeneration, rather than to the consequent transforming of their characters.

In the third passage the Word is a source of *wisdom* as it 'in-dwells' us (the same word is used as for the Spirit's indwelling). The conjunction of thoughts indicates that the word will only indwell 'richly' in the context of mutual instruction and united worship, i.e. of spiritual fellowship. This recalls Wesley's dictum that there is nothing more un-Christian than solitary Christianity.

27 : Life through the Word

James 1.16–25

The New Testament descriptions of God's *logos*, His 'discourse' or 'message', make a fascinating study. The *logos* of God's grace in Acts 20.32, and the *logos* of Christ in Col. 3.16, here appear as the *logos* of truth (18; so called because it tells of reality and is 'no lie' (cf. 3.14; 5.19; Col. 1.5; 1 John 2.21, 27). In v. 25 this *logos* is called God's 'perfect law', i.e. His full and final instruction in the way of life, in contrast with the incompleteness of the Old Testament *logos*. It is also called 'the law of liberty', the message that brings freedom where the Old Testament law had led to bondage. The thought that through God's sovereign action the message regenerates (18) is the same thought that Paul focuses when in Phil. 2.16 he calls the message 'the *logos* of life'.

God brought Christians to birth through the Word (18). James says this to illustrate the principle of v. 17, that all good things come from 'the Father of lights', the unchanging Creator of sun, moon and stars, whose ordering of the universe is the measure of His power to bless (cf. v. 25), and who through Christ shows Christians a Father's love (cf. v. 27; 3.9). As God's born-again children, Christians are the 'first-fruits' of creation in the sense of being that part which is given to God to be His sole possession and to be partaker of His holiness (cf. Exod. 23.19; Lev. 23.10–17;

35

Jer. 2.3). These are the dimensions of the new dignity and destiny into which the Word introduces us.

God brings men to glory through the Word (21). 'Souls' are persons; 'save' looks on to the last day (cf. 4.12). Here James states what v. 19 assumed, namely, that all depends on whether we are 'quick to hear' and receive the Word with meekness (i.e. humble acceptance, as from God), so that it becomes 'implanted' in the soil of our hearts. (Is there a capsuled reference in this image to Matt. 13.1–9, 18–23?) Our receptiveness, in turn, depends on our total moral state—whether we are willing to clamp down on our pride and other forms of natural nastiness or not (19–21). If we are, the Word can save us both here and hereafter.

God blesses those who are doers of the Word (25). A religion of hearing and not doing is hypocrisy and self-deceit. To forget our needs which God's message exposes is frivolous, stupid and inexcusable (23 f.). To look into the Word closely ('peer in' is what the Greek suggests), and to persevere in doing what it says, is the only way to be blessed.

Questions and themes for study and discussion on Studies 23-27

1. Is it biblically correct to call the Bible the Word of God? How can this description be justified?
2. What is the relation between the Spirit and the Word of God in (*a*) the new birth and (*b*) Christian obedience?
3. What does it mean to meditate on God's Word? Find some biblical examples. How is meditation related to prayer?
4. What is the place of the mind in the Christian life?
5. How does our moral condition affect our capacity to receive God's Word?
6. Spell out what it means to be 'blessed' by God.

SIX

Prayer and Life in Christ

28 : Help!

Psalm 31

Strangely and sadly, many Christian people regard quiet contemplation of God as a higher form of prayer than making requests. Luther disposed of this idea long ago by observing that no activity so fully honours God as bringing Him our needs and asking for His help; for hereby we declare that, contrary to what we would like to think, we are not self-sufficient and cannot be self-reliant, but depend on Him at every point for all that is good. Scripture shows that all true prayer has woven into it some kind of cry for help. Often prayer is more than this, but never less, for our need and dependence are constant. True prayer is born of need.

Pain of body and mind, and the sense of isolation through hostility, are experiences which bring home helplessness and need with special force. Hence many of the model forms in God's prayer-book (for that is what the psalter is) are cries for help springing from these experiences (22; see Pss. 3, 6, 22, 25, 30, 35, 38, 41–43, 55–57, 59, 62, 64, 69–71, 77, 88, 102, 109, 120, 142, 143). Psalm 31 is typical of this group in illustrating two basic lessons—how much we need to pray, and how blessed we are to have a God who heeds our prayers.

Note the *covenant relationship* which David's prayer invokes. Ten times he speaks of God by His covenant name, Yahweh, 'the LORD'. He calls Him '*my* God', '*my* rock, fortress, refuge' (14, 3 f.), and himself '*thy* servant' (16), and these personal pronouns are covenant language, signifying the mutual commitment wherein the relationship consists. He asks God, his faithful redeemer (5), to save him (1 f., 16) in His *righteousness*—faithfulness to His promise (1)—in His *steadfast love*—mercy sustained in covenant (16)—and for His *name's sake*—because He is Yahweh, David's covenant God (3).

Note too the *confident reliance* which David's prayer expresses. Recognizing that he is wholly in God's hand (15), he 'trusts' and 'calls on' God (6, 14, 17) to save him from weakness within

37

(9 f.) and malice without (11, 13, 15, 20 f.), fully confident from past experiences (7 f., 21 f.) that God can and will do it, and freely urging other saints to 'wait for the LORD' (24) as he himself is doing. The covenant is the basis for the confidence.

The incarnate Son of God, the pattern of human perfection, was a praying man, and part of v. 5 was on His lips when He died (Luke 23.46). Surely the whole substance of the psalm was in His heart, just as it should be in ours.

29 : Father

Luke 11.1–13

The *necessity* of prayer, which the disciples assumed in asking Jesus to teach them to pray (1), is explained by Jesus' reply. Reason one for praying is our *needs:* through asking we receive (9 f., 13); those who do not ask do not have (cf. Jas. 4.2). Reason two, more basic, is our *relationship with God*. We are to think of Him, and pray to Him, as our heavenly Father (2, 11 ff.), because in Christ He has adopted us (John 1.12 f.). But fathers want their children to have a meaningful relationship with them, and this is supremely true of God, who both made and redeemed us so that we might know, love, and enjoy Him. So God's deepest reason for requiring us to deal with Him in prayer is that thereby we might get to know Him better. We should realise that as the Giver is more important than His gifts, so the gifts are given to draw us nearer to the Giver. Every experience of answered prayer should bind us closer to God.

The Lord's Prayer, here given in a shorter form than in Matt. 6.9–13 (RSV text in vs. 2–4 is right), is a complete answer to the disciples' request, for it provides the *perfect pattern* for all Christian praying. God must come first: we are to ask for the supply of our material and spiritual needs (3 f.) only as means to, and in the way that will further, the hallowing of His name and the coming of His Kingdom (2)—in short, His glory; and we must recognize that He will only answer prayers concerning our own needs in the way that actually makes for His glory. 'Daily bread' covers all material needs; forgiveness and protection ('temptation' means a *testing* which shows up weaknesses) cover all spiritual needs. Note that vs. 5–8 relate directly to the former petition, and 11–13 to the latter.

How should we pray? *Urgently*, because of our need, and *expectantly*, because of our heavenly Father's goodness. This is the point made by the parables (i.e. *comparisons*, which is what 'parable' literally means in Greek) in vs. 5–13.

Light on *'unanswered'* prayer is suggested by vs. 11 f. If a son asks for a serpent or scorpion (something bad for him), will not his father give him a fish or an egg (something good for him)? God reserves the right to give the best, and to answer the prayers we should have made when those which we have made are awry. 2 Cor. 12.7–10 shows how this may work out.

30 : All Together

Acts 4.23–31

No doubt the early Christians had held prayer meetings before (cf. 1.14; 2.42, 46), but this is the first one to be described for us.

'Free' prayer meetings are a basic form of Christian fellowship. Talking together to God, as these Christians did (24), should be as natural and spontaneous as talking together with one another. Prayer together for each other's needs should always be part of the pattern which the church fulfils of mutual support and help (cf. 29; 12.5; Eph. 6.18–20). Hearts united in praying, and then in praising when prayer is answered, are God's delight (2 Cor. 1.11). Jesus promised that special heed will be paid to prayers which express the agreed mind of (at least) two Christians (Matt. 18.19). To practise togetherness in prayer is a Christian duty, and should be a Christian joy.

This particular prayer meeting, and the line along which the Christians prayed, were a reaction to threats from officialdom (21). As always in biblical praying, they built on the reality of God's dominion, as Maker and Lord of all (24, 28), and with this on the Spirit-given revelation which He has embodied in Holy Scripture (25–27)—in this case, the revelation that the rulers of this world regularly oppose the king whom God has anointed (Psa. 2.1 f.). They prayed, not in hope of getting this situation changed, but in order to gain strength to live and serve God in it. Strikingly, therefore, they asked, not for an abating of the threats or leave of absence from Jerusalem, but for boldness to proclaim the word in face of opposition, and for further confirmation of their witness to Jesus' lordship of the kind given when the lame man was healed (29 f.; **3.**1–10). They were thinking not of their own safety, but of the cause of God. '*Thy* will be done; *thy* kingdom come.'

It was the right prayer, and it was wonderfully answered. Pentecost almost came again! They felt the place 'shaken', in token of vast divine energy being let loose, and with the Spirit's power strong in them they witnessed boldly, just as they had asked that they might (31). Prayer for boldness in witness will always be answered positively, if we dare to make it. (But do we?)

31 : His Name, and His Will

John 16.23–27; 1 John 5.13–17

These two passages are profound and hard to grasp, for they lead deeper into the realities of prayer than most of us have ever gone.

Both show that the supreme experience of prayer into which our heavenly Father wants to draw us is not mystical ecstasy (some taste this, some do not), but is rather the joy—and joy it is (John **16.**24)—of *receiving what we have asked for.* We find this joy, however, only as we learn to ask aright. The aim of prayer is not to force God's hand or make Him do our will against His own, but to deepen our knowledge of Him, and our fellowship with Him, through contemplating His glory, confessing our dependence and need, and consciously embracing His goals. Our asking, therefore, must be *according to God's will* (1 John **5.**14), and *in Jesus' name* (John **16.**23 f., cf. **14.**13; **15.**7, 16)—that is, it must express knowledge of both God's *goals* and His *grace*.

The context of such asking is *assured* faith. It belongs to 'that day' (John **16.**23), when Jesus is risen and enthroned, and the Spirit has come, giving men 'understanding' to know God and eternal life (1 John **5.**20, 13), and convincing them that the love they saw in Jesus is the Father's love for them too (John **16.**27). In that day, when Jesus by the Spirit teaches them 'plainly' of the Father (25), no question of enlisting Jesus' support in prayer, as if He was more merciful than the Father or could influence the Father in a way they could not, will arise (26); for they will know that they, as believers, are the Father's beloved (27)— which is what Christian assurance is all about (cf. Rom. **8.**38 f.).

40

To ask *in Jesus' name* is not to use a verbal spell, but to invoke a personal solidarity. We base our asking on Christ's saving relationship to us through the cross, and we make petitions which Christ, as we know Him, can endorse and put His name to—'that the Father may be glorified in the Son' (John **14.**13). Then, when the Father answers, He gives 'in Jesus' name' (**16.**23, RSV)—that is, *through* Jesus as our mediator and *to* Jesus as the one who will be glorified, to His Father's glory, through what is given to us, Jesus' servants.

Central in the life of prayer is seeking to be taught by Christ through His word and Spirit what we should pray for. Sometimes we are permitted to know this more specifically than at other times and in other matters. 1 John **5.**16 is an example of Christ-taught, Spirit-prompted prayer ('mortal sin', RSV, being apostasy). To the extent that we *know*, through the Spirit's inner witness, that we are making a request which the Lord has specifically given us to make, to that extent we *know* that we have the answer, even before we see it. If all this is a closed book to you, deal with God about it today.

32 : Praying for Christians

Colossians 1.3–14

Paul regularly prayed for Christians, and asked them to pray for him (see Rom. **1.**9, **15.**30; 2 Cor. **1.**11; Eph. **1.**16 ff., **3.**14 ff., **6.**18 ff.; Phil. **1.**4–11; 1 Thess. **1.**2, **5.**25; 2 Thess. **3.**1; 2 Tim. **1.**3; Philem. 4 ff., 22). Praying for fellow Christians is a basic Christian responsibility. This passage helps us see how to discharge it.

Paul prays in terms of his knowledge of God's goal. The formula being applied in all his prayers is 'thy will be done'. From hearing of the Colossians' faith in Christ, love in the Spirit to Christians, and hope prompting both (4 f., 8), he knows they have been caught up in God's saving purpose (cf. 1 Thess. **1.**3 ff., where Paul appears to infer election from faith, hope and love). So he prays that all God's purpose for Christians may be fulfilled in their lives, and asks God to give them four things:

1. *Christian knowledge*—knowledge of God's will (His plans, ways and commands) and of God Himself (9 f.). The Greek word used implies *full, thorough* knowledge, as does the verb 'filled'. In v. 9, 'understanding' relates to principles of truth,

41

'wisdom' to application of those principles in life. The construction of v. 10 shows that worthy living depends on this knowledge: he who does not know God's will cannot do it. Knowledge of God increases as one lives up to what one has already (10, cf. Mark 4.24 f.).

2. *Christian practice*—a life worthy of Christ the King (13), to whom we owe our salvation (14); a life pleasing God at every point and by every activity (10).

3. *Christian patience*—cheerful endurance of trying people and situations, with actual rejoicing as tribulation grinds on (11). Not for nothing does Paul specify that all God's strength and power and might are needed to produce such a reaction!

4. *Christian thankfulness*—gratitude for grace, the major motive of Christian living. According to 'the truth of the gospel' (5), Christian doctrine is grace and Christian ethics is gratitude, all the way.

33 : The Power of Prayer

James 5.13–18

Christians, says James, should pray for *themselves* when in trouble (13). Why? Because in prayer we look up from our distresses to gaze on God, the merciful Potentate who will in due course deliver His suffering servants (11). Thus prayer brings stability and strength; seeing temporal problems in eternal perspective cuts them down to size (cf. Psa. 73; Rom. 8.18; 2 Cor. 4.7–18).

Christians should equally pray for *other Christians* when they are in trouble (14–16). Invalids may ask that their pastors pray over them; elders must be ready to do this on request (14). This is not, of course, a magic formula for a cure: while Jesus' miracles show that there is indeed bodily healing for us in the atonement (cf. Matt. 8.17), Jesus' attitude to Paul's thorn in the flesh (2 Cor. 12.7–10) indicates that it is not His will for every Christian always to enjoy perfect health in this body—though when we get our new one it will be different! But we must be clear that the benefits of the atonement are one thing, God's time and manner for conveying them is another. Solemn prayer over the whole range of the invalid's needs is what James counsels, on the principle that illness is always God's summons to consider one's ways.

Such prayer may well issue in a healing which, like that of the paralytic in Mark 2.3–12, is a clear act of God, and proof of forgiveness (15). This will show the power, not of the oil used to designate the person whom God was asked to bless, but of the prayer itself. Such prayer for each other's spiritual wellbeing ('healing') should not be limited to Christian invalids (16).

'Faith' (15) means, not passive orthodoxy, as in James' *ad hominem* discussion of what 'a man' may say in 2.14–26 (see vs. 14, 18, 20), but active trust, just as in 1.6 and in Paul. James and Paul differ in cast of mind, but not in doctrine.

The efficacy of prayer depends on (*a*) uprightness of life and motive (16, cf. 4.3), and (*b*) whole-hearted and sustained earnestness (17, cf. 1.5–8) in the person praying, plus (*c*) congruity of the prayer with God's revealed purposes and ways (cf. Study 31). The story of Elijah (17 f.) illustrates (*a*) and (*b*) explicitly (cf. 1 Kings 17.1, 18.42) and (*c*) by implication (cf. Deut. 11.13–17).

Questions and themes for study and discussion on Studies 28-33

1. Why pray? List the reasons.
2. Do some prayers go unanswered? If so, why?
3. How should the Lord's Prayer be used in the Christian's personal life?
4. What can be said in favour of prayer meetings, and what do you think is the ideal form for them?
5. How should a Christian test whether he prays in the name of Jesus?
6. Under what circumstances can we speak of 'the prayer of faith'?
7. What is the work of the Holy Spirit in relation to Christian prayer?

SEVEN

The Indwelling Spirit

34 : The Gift of the Spirit

John 14.15–18; 1 John 3.19–24

Before Christ came, God's Spirit was active in creation (Gen. 1.2), revelation (cf. 1 Pet. 1.10 f.), and regeneration (Psa. 51.10 f.). When Jesus said that following His departure (John 14.25 f.) His Father would give the disciples the Spirit, His meaning was that the Spirit would then start ministering to them in a new way. He would be *with* them (16), *by their side* (17, as Weymouth renders the words translated 'with you' in the RSV), and *in* them (17), as 'another Counsellor' (16, RSV), taking Jesus' place. 'Counsellor' is *parakletos*, a word with a wider meaning than any English rendering can catch; carrying the basic idea of 'one called alongside to help', it is used for an advocate at law and for anyone acting as friend, supporter and encourager ('comforter' in the old, strong AV sense). This is a personal ministry—which shows that the Spirit is not just a power, but a person, like Jesus, who sustained the Counsellor's role before the Spirit assumed it.

The phrase 'Spirit of truth' points to what is distinctive in the Spirit's new ministry: He shows Christians the truth about the glory of the ascended Lord, who is Truth in person (6), and so makes Him glorious in their eyes (16.14). Moreover, He mediates communion between them and Christ, who through the Spirit's coming 'comes' to His people on earth (18). Rutherford's testimony from prison, 'Christ came into my cell last night', is the best commentary on this. Here, rather than in any outward manifestations, is the heart of the Spirit's pentecostal ministry— the ministry in virtue of which He is called the Spirit of Christ (Rom. 8.9, where the small 's' in some editions of the RSV is wrong).

This ministry is permanent (16): the Spirit dwells with, and is in, Jesus' disciples for ever (17). ('Know' and 'dwell' in v. 17 are probably future in meaning: the present tense can be used this way in Greek.) There is, however, an ethical condition of enjoying the Spirit's ministry: those who will not keep Christ's commandments are disqualified (15, cf. 1 John 3.24).

The verses from 1 John appeal to the gift of the indwelling Spirit as proof that God (or, perhaps, the Son of God) indwells us. How do we know we have this gift? By experience of the Spirit's ministry of showing us Jesus' glory and drawing us into fellowship with Him. One who knows, loves and serves Jesus certainly has the Spirit.

35 : The Spirit's Law of Life

Romans 8.1–17

Having announced the theme of 'the new life of the Spirit' (Rom. 7.6), and then postponed it in order to discuss the way in which the law exposes sin without empowering for righteousness (7.7–25), Paul now develops a classic account of the Spirit's ministry to believers.

'Law' in the phrase 'the Spirit's law of life' (2) seems to mean 'principle', almost 'mode of action', as in 7.23. This 'law', working through the gospel, frees Christians now from sin's penalty and power, and will one day free them from sin's presence within them. Sin's *penalty* is done away through Christ's atoning sacrifice which fully met sin's claim, so that now there is 'no condemnation for those that are in Christ Jesus' (1–4a). Sin's *power* has ceased to dominate us (cf. 6.14), for we are in the Spirit, indwelt by the Spirit, walking in the Spirit, and 'minding' the things of the Spirit, i.e. the realities which the Spirit makes known (9, 4, 5). Those 'in the flesh' are strangers to this life, but believers are not in the flesh any more (4b–9). Sin's *presence* is recalled when Paul speaks of our bodies being 'dead' (doomed to death) through sin: we are reminded of his analysis of life in 'this body of death' (7.24), where sin, dethroned but not yet destroyed, still indwells and marauds (7.14 ff.). But one day the Spirit will quicken our bodies in resurrection, conforming them to Christ's (cf. Phil. 3.21), and then our vulnerability to sin will be gone for good (10 f.). (And won't it be good!)

On this basis, Paul requires his readers (12 f.) here and now to 'mortify the deeds of the body'—that is, do sinful habits to death—through letting the Spirit bring to bear on them 'the things of the Spirit', notably, knowledge of the purpose and

45

power of the Lord Jesus, and of the new life He has given (cf. Col. 3.1–6). This prompts him to speak of two further ministries of the Spirit to God's children. The first is *leading* them in the way of holiness and mortification of sin (14)—a ministry whereby He shows them to be sons of God. The second is *witnessing* to their adoption and heirship in their own consciousness (15 f.), so that instinctively they look to God as their Father and hope for His glory. Paul's 'I am persuaded' (38 f.) is a partial voicing of the 'triumphing assurance' that the Spirit's witness brings; in a fuller sense, the whole chapter is voicing it.

36 : Walk in the Spirit
Galatians 5.13–26

Galatians declares how Christians have exchanged the bondage of legal religion for the freedom of life in the Spirit (2.19 f.; 3.2 f.; 5.1, 5 f., 13; 6.15). Not by works but by faith—not by the law but by the Spirit—not by circumcision but by new creation—not in bondage but in freedom—these are the antitheses on which Paul's argument about the making of Christians turns. Here he adds a further antithesis about the conduct ('walk', 16, 25) of Christians: be led, he says, not by the flesh but by the Spirit. 'Flesh' (16, 17, 19, 24) means, not our bodies or humanity as such, but the 'indwelling sin' of Rom. 7.7–25, the energy of our fallenness in Adam. Paul's main points are these:

1. *The commitment of the Christian brings conflict.* Christians have denied what the Puritans called 'carnal self' in order to be 'led by the Spirit' (18); they have 'crucified the flesh' (24) in the sense of renouncing its ways, wishing it dead, and asking Jesus to kill it. This is the essence of repentance. But conflict arises at once, for the flesh, though doomed, is not dead yet. Desires prompted by the indwelling Spirit, and impulses springing from sin (including distaste for the Spirit's promptings) pull against each other (cf. Rom. 7.14–25 again), so that the Christian is never free from a degree of inner tension and frustration. The last words of v. 17 do not mean that he cannot do any good that he would, only that he can never do enough of it to satisfy him and always achieves less than he hoped for, inasmuch as somewhere within him the brakes went on and the steering-wheel of motive and purpose got twisted.

46

2. *The indwelling of the Spirit brings Christlikeness.* Refusing to gratify the flesh (16) is the negative side of sanctification; its positive side is the building up of Christian character and habits, with love to one's neighbour crowning everything (22 f., 13 f.). 'Fruit' is singular, for the nine graces mentioned unite to form one thing, the image of Jesus (cf. 2 Cor. 3.18). Paul's metaphor embodies the thought that the Christlikeness which the Spirit enables us to exhibit reveals the new creation in Christ of our innermost self, that transforming work of grace whereby the bad tree was made capable of producing good fruit (see Matt. 7.17 f.; 12.33).

37 : Gratify the Spirit

Ephesians 4.25–32; 5.15–20

In Ephesians God's gift of the indwelling Spirit is pictured as His 'seal' set upon Christians to mark them out as His (cf. 2 Cor. 1.22). The picture points forward to the day when God will claim His property, thus sealed, and take believers out of the realm of sin and death for ever (Eph. 1.13 f.; 4.30). The word 'redemption', meaning 'rescue' and implying a ransom, is used of this hope in 4.30, as in Rom. 8.23, though its commoner reference is to present forgiveness through the cross, as in Eph. 1.7.

In the first three chapters, Paul spoke of the Spirit's work in giving knowledge of God (1.17; 3.5, 16–19) and fellowship with Him (2.18, 22); in the last three, the burden of all references to the Spirit is ethical.

The plea against *grieving* the Spirit (4.30) is a witness both to the Spirit's personality and to the fact that divine holiness is His nature (which is why He is called the *Holy* Spirit). As with the first and second Persons of the Godhead, so with the third— some ways of behaving please Him, others distress and offend Him. In the second category come the lapses mentioned in v. 31, and stealing (28), and in short all transgressions of the moral law. For Christians to fall into these sins grieves the Spirit because it directly thwarts His purpose and spoils His work of making us Christlike. Knowledge that our bodies are temples of the Holy Spirit (1 Cor. 6.19), and that this 'gracious, willing Guest' is hard at work in our hearts to sanctify us, should induce the 'fear and trembling' of Phil. 2.12 ('reverent awe' is the meaning) and quickly shame us out of any moral laxity.

To this dissuasive against grieving the Spirit the call to be *filled* with the Spirit (5.18) is the positive counterpart. The imperative is in the present tense, implying a constant obligation. 'Filled' conveys the thought of being wholly concerned with, and wholly controlled by, the realities which the Spirit makes known, and the ideal of life to which He points us. The question which vs. 18–20 raise and answer is, from what source should satisfaction be sought? Not from indulgence in alcohol (the worldling's way of trying to raise his enjoyment level), but from being occupied entirely with the Spirit's concerns. Then we shall have something to sing about! (19)—for the gratified Holy Spirit will sustain in us a joy which the worldling never knows (cf. Rom. 14.17).

Questions and themes for study and discussion on Studies 34-37

1. What differences, if any, were there between the Holy Spirit's ministry to the apostles and His ministry to us?
2. How does the Spirit bear witness to us that we are children of God?
3. How from the Scriptures would you counsel a Christian who wanted to be filled with the Holy Spirit?
4. Under what conditions can one claim to be 'led by the Spirit'?
5. 'Honour the Holy Spirit' (Evan Roberts). What do these passages suggest to you in the way of steps to be taken by those who would do as Roberts said?

EIGHT

Christian Fellowship

38 : Love One Another
John 13.34–35; 1 John 3.10–18

Jesus told His disciples to love each other (John 13.34; 1 John 3.11). But love is an elastic and problematical word; what should 'loving' involve? Jesus answered this question, and set the sights of Christian love for all time, by adding: 'as I have loved you'. The measures of love are how much it gives, how free it is from selfish motives, how much it puts up with, and how long it lasts. Jesus' love gave to the uttermost (for Him, the cost of loving was Calvary). It was totally selfless (look at Gethsemane). It was infinitely patient (Jesus' sweetness with His silly disciples is breathtaking). And it was, and is, unending. This is the Christian standard. It is from Calvary alone that we 'know love' (1 John 3.16); only at Calvary are love's deepest dimensions understood. That is why the command to imitate Christ's love is 'new' (John 13.34). Such love was undreamed-of before.

Love is fundamental to fellowship, for fellowship consists precisely of giving and taking, and only those who love as Jesus did can give of themselves in the way that fellowship requires.

In the 1 John passage the apostle casts this commandment, as he does so much else, into a test of life. He who does not love his brother (i.e. his fellow Christian) is thereby shown to be a child, not of God, but of the devil (10–12). Like Cain, and the world generally (13), he hates godly men because they make him feel uncomfortable, and hate is murder before God (cf. Matt. 5.21 f.) whether it breaks out in murderous action or not (15). John's antithesis is inexorable and ultimately inescapable: if you do not love, then you hate.

John adds two practical points. The first concerns assurance. From finding in ourselves love of the brethren, we know by infallible inference, that we have passed from spiritual death to spiritual life—for one cannot love all Christians as such without being spiritually alive (14). The second point detects hypocrisy. Love is more than talk; it is action for the relief of need (17 f.). Only action of this kind is love 'in truth' (i.e. reality) (18).

39 : Sharing

Acts 2.43–47; 4.32–37

Pentecost loosed into the world a new quality of corporate life, marked by an exuberant riot of caring and sharing and an infectious joy (2.46), which overthrew all inhibitions about going to the limit to help others. This was *fellowship* (2.42)—*koinonia*, literally 'having things in common'. In v. 46, '*generous* hearts' (RSV) is a good interpretation of 'singleness'—single-minded concentration on giving, as a mark of love, is the meaning intended. Though spontaneous in expression, the new life-style was not uncaused: it issued from the Spirit's new covenant ministry, making the love and power of Christ vividly real. Fellowship between Christians always comes about through conscious realization of Christ's own fellowship with each of them (cf. 1 John 1.3).

As praise is both a Christian instinct (2.47) and a duty, so with togetherness (cf. 2.44; 4.32). Heb. 3.13; 10.24 f., present meeting and mutual ministry as a duty, but here togetherness in worship, at table and at other times (2.46 f.), is recorded simply as a fact. The RSV is right in 4.23 to interpret 'their own people' (the literal meaning) as 'friends': that is how Christians saw each other in those days of spiritual vigour, and friends do not usually need to be told to get together!

The ancient world by and large was callous towards poverty, but the first practical expression of Christian fellowship was to pool resources for poor relief (2.45; 4.32, 34 ff.). For the first time ever Marx's maxim, 'From each according to his ability; to each according to his need', became the rule of action. The maxim, which came to Marx from Christian sources, is, of course, profoundly right, but only where Christ is Lord can there be motive force enough to live it out. The poverty of the Jerusalem saints twenty-five years later (cf. Rom. 15.25–27) may suggest that from one standpoint this experiment in communal Christianity was injudicious: it may have reflected an incautious assumption that because Jesus' return is certain (cf. Acts 3.20) therefore it must be soon (cf. the Thessalonian mistake, 2 Thess. 2.1 f.; 3.6–12). Paul's charge to the rich (1 Tim. 6.17 ff.) shows that there is another way of being a faithful steward of property than selling up. But the Christian good-heartedness of Barnabas, who sold his entire estate for charity, is not to be faulted; it is a model for us all (4.36 f.).

40 : Welcome!

Romans 15.1–13

The gospel invitation to mankind is, in the words of a Bunyan book title, 'come and welcome to Jesus Christ'. The Church's invitation to believers must always be, 'come and welcome into the fellowship of those whom Christ has welcomed' (7).

In Rom. 14.1–15.13, Paul argues that Christians must receive each other with the same full acceptance, the same concern for the other's welfare, and the same forbearance of the other's weaknesses, as Christ showed in receiving them. So we must bear with each other's oddities and scruples about food and drink, Sabbath-keeping, and other areas where Christian liberty and discretion come in (14.1–12); we must not let our freedom be another's stumbling-block (14.13–23); like Christ, the archetypal Servant (15.8), we must forgo the luxury of pleasing ourselves, so that our neighbour may be edified and God's cause maintained (2 f.). Jew and Gentile in particular must fully receive each other in Christ, for Scripture is explicit that Christ came to save both (7–13).

It is worth asking how this bears on (a) racially or sociologically selective congregations and (b) intercommunion between denominational groups.

As Paul develops his theme, three other truths come in as a kind of bass line:

1. *Scripture's purpose is to encourage Christians.* Having cited Psa. 69.9 in v. 3, and intending to cite Psa. 18.49; Deut. 32.43; Psa. 117.1; and Isa. 11.10 (vs. 9–12), to show that Jesus' ministry to the Gentiles was foretold no less than His rejection by the Jews, Paul is led to make the great generalization of v. 4. He spoke of the Old Testament only; how much more do his words fit the New! To show us Christ and God's promises (8) for our encouragement is the basic use of the whole Bible.

2. *Christian character is God's gift*: steadfastness, courage, hope, joy, peace, faith (5, 13) come through the word (4) and Spirit (13) alone.

3. *The goal of grace is the praise of God*, by those to whom grace came (6, 7, 9, 11, cf. Eph. 1.6, 12, 14). So now; so for ever.

Nor are these truths irrelevant to the main theme; for Christian welcoming will be most in evidence where the giving of God is best known, and the worship of God best practised.

51

41 : Burden-bearing

Galatians 6.1–6

Having in ch. 5 told his readers to walk in the Spirit and serve each other in love (5.16, 25, 13 f.), Paul here explains what this will mean. The law of Christ, he says, is precisely this—to bear others' burdens (2), accepting involvement in their troubles and laying oneself out to help, support and restore (1). It pleases God more that I should carry someone else's burden and let him carry mine than that we should each carry our own. The latter is the way of lonely isolation, one aspect of the fallen human condition; the former is the way of Christian fellowship. Fellowship means sharing burdens as well as benefits: we carry each other's luggage, both material and spiritual, and find relief and strength in doing so. This path of exchange—problem-sharing and burden-bearing—is Christ's image in our lives, for it reflects His loving substitution for us under judgement on the cross. '*O Christ, what burdens bowed Thy head; my load was laid on Thee.*'

Paul summons his readers to the burden-bearing life as his *brothers* in Christ (in 4.19 he had called them his children!) and as *spiritual* men, indwelt and led by the Spirit of God. It is to this life of fellowship in action that sonship in God's family commits us (cf. 1 Pet. 3.8), and for this that the Spirit is given to equip us.

Paul weaves together two lines of exhortation: with the call to burden-bearing goes a warning against complacent conceit (1b, 3–5). Psychologically this is shrewd; those who seek to do good (10), especially in counselling and rescue work (1), are always tempted to feel they are a cut above those they are helping. 'Gentleness', as distinct from the overbearing attitude which betrays superiority feelings, is called for here, since 'there but for the grace of God go I' (cf. v. 1; 1 Cor. 10.12). Paul reminds us that the 'load' each man must carry (nothing to do with the burden-bearing of v. 2) is his responsibility for his own life, for which he must answer to God, to reap what he has sown (5, 7 ff.); so each of us will be wise to 'test his own work' (4), and not rest in the thought that some are a lot worse than he is.

The injunction of v. 6, so comforting to preachers, is not as isolated from Paul's theme as it looks. How else, when pastors are impoverished (and they often are), should the rule of burden-bearing be applied?

42 : Love that Hurts

1 Thessalonians 2.17–3.10

Following a three-week mission Paul left his Thessalonian converts in a hurry, for the Jews and the mob were demonstrating against him (Acts 17.1–10). The circumstances made persecution certain, and though Paul had told them to expect this (3.4) he feared that, being young in the faith and as yet imperfectly instructed (10) they would not have resources to cope with it (3). So he soon sent Timothy to them from Athens to support and strengthen them (1 f.). Timothy brought back good news of them—Paul's verb in v. 6 is that which he normally uses for preaching the 'good news' of the gospel—and Paul, in joy, at once wrote the letter from which this passage comes. (Incidentally, it should be read as one paragraph; the chapter division is inappropriate.) It is worth remembering that Paul's readers were perhaps a year old in the faith, but hardly more.

Pastoral love, whereby an older Christian feels and carries responsibility for other and particularly for younger Christians, is one of the costliest forms of Christian fellowship. All Christians will have some such responsibility; pastoral love is regularly required of us all, not just of ministers in pastorates. Pastoral love brings deep concern and makes one deeply vulnerable: not being able to meet those whom one loves (2.17 f.; 3.6, 10), not knowing how they are managing under pressure (5), not knowing even whether one's love is returned (6; cf. 2 Cor. 6.11–13; 12.14 f.), hurts. As a rule, those who love most are hurt most. There is, of course, another side: pastoral love blossoms into joy and pride when the loved ones make progress (2.19 f.; 3.8), and the more love the more joy. Paul knows that it is God, not himself, whom he must thank for his converts' faith and faithfulness (7–9; 1.2); but the joy he has in the knowledge that he has not, under God, laboured in vain (3.5) is real and honest and nothing to be ashamed of 'before our God' (9). To know that God has used you to bless others in a decisive way, is joy indeed.

So far from exploiting the loved ones in its own interest, pastoral love identifies with their interests and is all at their disposal. So Paul prays, and is ready to work again, for his converts' spiritual welfare (10–13; 2.18; 1.2). It is to encourage them that Paul sweetly tells them how the news of their steadfastness had ministered encouragement to him (7 f.).

43 : The Way of Fellowship

1 John 1

John's first letter is the classic New Testament treatment of fellowship. Two paragraphs form its first chapter. Verses 1–4 are John's *preamble*, stating why he is writing; vs. 5–10 give his *principles*, which determine the letter's content. 'That you may have fellowship with us' is the purpose (3), and the principles are these:

Axiom—God is wholly *light*; that is, purity and holiness are what He is, what He demands, and what He gives (5). (In the way that He gives it He shows Himself to be love too [4.8–10].) Hence follow four corollaries:

1. Those who walk (live) in darkness (impurity and unholiness) have no fellowship with God (6).

2. Those who walk in the light enjoy fellowship with each other and cleansing, through Christ before God, so that nothing disrupts traffic between them and Him (7).

3. Those who deny their sins are truth-less and self-deceived, contradicting God (8, 10).

4. Those who acknowledge their sins receive forgiveness and cleansing from God (9).

The rest of the letter rings changes on these principles.

Fellowship with God for John is a love-traffic of receiving from Him and giving to Him. We enter it through receiving apostolic witness to Christ (1.3, 5), which the Spirit enables us to do (2.20, 27). John elucidates the relationship in terms of:

(*a*) *Living*: having 'life', 'the life', 'that eternal life' which is in Jesus the Son, and which indeed Jesus Himself is (1.1 f.; 5.11–13, 20).

(*b*) *Knowing* God, Father and Son (1.3; 5.20), and the love of both (4.16, 3.16). This involves acknowledging the realities of the Son's incarnation as Jesus the Christ (4.2) and His atoning death ('blood') (1.7, cf. 2.2; 4.9 f.)—otherwise one 'has' neither the Son nor the Father (2.22 f.).

(*c*) *Loving* God for His love, and so obeying and abiding in Him (2.5, 15; 4.19; 5.2 f.).

(*d*) *Receiving* God's gifts in answer to prayer (3.22; 5.14–16).

Fellowship with Christians means loving them in a practical way (3.18)—providing for their needs (3.17), and praying for them (cf. 5.16). It is a relationship presupposing personal fellow-

54

ship with the Father and the Son on the part of each individual involved (1.3).

Questions and themes for study and discussion on Studies 38-43

1. In what ways does the command, 'Love one another as I have loved you', mark an advance on Old Testament ethics?
2. In the light of Study 38, how far should a church go in looking after the material needs of its members?
3. How can one love and live in fellowship with persons of a different background to oneself, whom one does not like?
4. Think out ways in which the principle of bearing one another's burdens can and should be applied.
5. Can one be in fellowship with another Christian without having thereby some pastoral responsibility for him?
6. What does it mean to 'walk in the light'?

NINE

The Christian in the World

44 : Be Different

Deuteronomy 6.10–15; 12.29–32

God's world, having rejected its Maker, is always at cross purposes with His people. This must be frankly faced; we dare not be starry-eyed about it. Such was Moses' message to Israel, standing poised to enter Canaan. In Canaan, he says, you will be tempted to become like the locals, and like your neighbours, but you are called to be nonconformists—indeed, separatists!—in relation to these things. Be different! or the God who is cutting off the Canaanites in judgement before you (12.29) will turn and destroy you as well (6.15).

Moses, like all good preachers, has three points:

1. *Don't forget the Lord* (6.12). He is a great and gracious benefactor (10 f.), a strong Saviour (12), and as He remembers His promise to give (10) so He expects us to remember our obligation to serve (12 f.). Sin and Satan, however, create absent-mindedness where God's deeds and claims are concerned (cf. Matt. 13.19; Jer. 2.32; 3.21; 13.25; 18.15). Today's pressures quickly obliterate the memory of yesterday's provision, and the very enjoyment of God's good gifts can divert our hearts from the Giver (10 ff.). The constant commemoration of God's works in the Psalms is a deliberate antidote to this (cf. Pss. 42.6; 77.11 f.; 105 5)—and such antidotes are always in season. The Passover and Lord's Supper were instituted as antidotes against forgetfulness, too (cf. Deut. 16.3; 1 Cor. 11.24 ff.).

2. *Don't divide your loyalty* (6.14). As a loving husband is rightly jealous that his wife's affection should be exclusively his, and will be justly angry if she plays him false, so with God (15). God's people, therefore, must play the faithful wife's role and keep themselves wholly for Him, as the first commandment requires (5.7; 6.4 f.). The 'fear' they must practise is, as always in Scripture, a combination of reverence, loyalty and love in response to covenant mercy (13). Swearing by God's name is a way of showing allegiance (13). (Jesus' attack on the mentality

that covers deceit with oaths [Matt. 5.33–37] does not contradict this; it is a different point.)

3. *Don't serve God in pagan ways* (12.30 f.). Barbarities which God hates in the service of superstition would be equally hateful in His own worship. It is obedience, not sacrifice (let alone human sacrifice) that He wants (32; cf. 1 Sam. 15.22). So curb your conformist cravings, attend to His word, and—be different!

45 : Salt and Light

Matthew 5.13–16; Ephesians 5.3–14

Jesus uses two parables (comparisons, illustrations) to show what influence His disciples should have in the world. First, the parable of *salt* (Matt. 5.13) teaches that they are to act as a preservative and a flavouring: that is, they should be a force making against rottenness and for wholeness in sin-sick society. This requires them to be *in* the world, not withdrawn from it (cf. John 17.15; 1 Cor. 5.10); for salt cannot preserve what it does not touch. It requires also that they be *different* from the world, for only so can they fulfil their own regenerate nature and do their appointed job. Salt that has lost its saltness is a useless mockery of itself: it is fit only to be thrown away. Finally, Jesus' figure suggests that Christians need not be discouraged when in a minority: a little real salt will preserve a lot of meat!

The parable of *light* teaches four main truths. First, God means the Christian community to be noticed. Just by existing, it should be calling attention to itself, like a city on a hill (14); if men can overlook it, something is wrong! Second, God means this community to enlighten the world. By being itself, and living its own life, it is to expose the shoddiness and unworthiness of the world's ways and display in practice what human existence is meant to be. Lights are not lit so that they may then be stopped from shining! (14 f.). Third, the community must be zealous and untiring in the practice of 'good works' (16, cf. Tit. 2.14): 'let your light shine'. Fourth, the community's exhibition of the Christian way of life is meant to move others to praise their God—and once people have begun to praise the Christian God for others' salvation, they may well before long be found going to Him to seek their own (16). Note that there is no disjunction here between deeds and words as alternative ways of witness, as the

57

'silent service' tend to suppose ('I witness by my life, not by talking'); Jesus' assumption is rather that verbal witness to the Christians' heavenly Father has already been borne (how else would watching worldlings know to praise Him?), and the 'good works' are now backing it up.

The Ephesians passage follows a parallel line of thought: 1. As light in the Lord, *avoid* the darkness of the world's ways (3–10). 2. As light in the Lord, *expose* that darkness (11 ff.), as your own new way of life cannot but do (9 f.). 3. As light in the Lord, you will thus *arouse* those who sleep in that darkness to receive the light of Christ (13 f.).

46 : Against Men

Matthew 10.16–42

This passage, the end of Jesus' charge to the twelve setting out to preach in Galilee (10.5 ff.), looks on to situations which would only develop later, when following post-Pentecostal clashes with the authorities serious persecution of Christians by their fellow Jews would start (cf. Acts 8.1 ff.). Three themes appear: do not trust men, but trust God (16–25); do not fear men, but fear God (26–33); do not follow your family, but follow Christ (34–42). Each section ends by focusing on Jesus' own place and ministry: first, as the divine Master whose lot His servants must be ready to share (24 f.); second, as the divine Son who in heaven will champion before His Father those who championed Him on earth (32 f.); third, as the divine Emissary who is received, as the God who sent Him is received, when His own representatives are received, and who will see that those who receive them are rewarded (40 ff.). Jesus' awareness of being Son of God, sent to be men's Teacher, King and Judge, is explicit here.

The first section says that disciples must be prepared for hatred (22) and persecution (17 f., 22 f., 25). Men will be 'wolves' for ferocity in opposing them (16), for the preaching of the gospel raises the antithesis between the world and God to its height. But the Spirit is promised for their defence, so they should not panic (19 f.). Verse 23 is enigmatic; perhaps Jesus meant it so. His coming to the throne through the ascension, of which evidence was given at Pentecost (cf. 26.64=Luke 22.69), or His coming to Jerusalem in judgement in A.D. 70 are both easier reference-points for the last phrase than is the Second Coming.

The second section says that disciples must not be daunted from proclaiming Christ by fear of men (26, 28, 31). For (*a*) God means the secret of the gospel to be blazoned abroad, so that its publishers are entirely in God's will (26 f.); (*b*) human foes cannot in any case kill the soul (28; the second half of the verse refers to God—not the devil!); (*c*) God knows and can protect disciples fully (29 f.); (*d*) Jesus will welcome faithful witnesses into glory (32 f.).

The third section says that disciples must expect division about Christ to invade their families, creating a clash of loyalties in which for Jesus' sake they must count the family as foes (34 ff.). This is painful: but no limit can be set to what a disciple must be ready to lose and suffer on the road to his reward (37 ff.).

47 : The Secret of Stickability

Hebrews 10.32–39; 12.1–4

Christians need 'stickability'—resilience, endurance, perseverance, patience (**10.36**; **12.1**; verb, **12.2, 3**)—for they live under constant pressure from the world around. Here, Jews and worldlings had put the boot in, and the Hebrew believers were pressed hard (32 ff.). As we noted earlier (Study 20) they were tempted to think that by abandoning their Christian profession and reverting to Judaism they could gain immunity without loss. This, however, was not so: those who give up Christ (29) lose everything, for they incur the black guilt and awful judgement of apostasy (26–31, cf. **6.4–8**). The letter was written to explain this to them, and to urge them to stand firm. Chapter **10.32–39** encourages them to keep on as they have been going, points to the promise of reward for those who patiently endure, and expresses confidence that they will qualify for that reward when Christ comes.

You need endurance, says the writer, and the secret of endurance is faith (35, 38 f.). He cites Hab. **2.3** f. to show that faith —meaning confident, hopeful trust in God and His promises (35, 38 f.; **11.1, 6**)—is that by which the godly man will live. Paul quotes Habakkuk's words to focus the thought that a man comes to be righteous (right) with God, and so to gain life, by receiving God's gift of righteousness through Christ (Rom. **1.17**; Gal. **3.11**); the anonymous writer to the Hebrews uses them to show that the godly man gains life by hoping in God's promise of reward through Christ. It should be noticed that faith, in Hebrews, includes what Paul distinguishes as hope, while faith, in Paul, includes what Hebrews distinguish as confidence (10.35). The implications of Habakkuk's statement in context are broad enough to justify both Paul's use of it and that in Hebrews.

As faith is the secret of endurance, so gazing at Jesus is the secret of faith. This is the point of 12.1–4. The Christian life is pictured as a race. To run it with endurance, we must first *lay aside* every 'weight' (retarding factor) and 'clinging sin' (i.e. unbelief, sluggishness, complacency: cf. 3.12 f.; 4.11; 6.12), and then *look above* to Jesus. He is faith's pioneer and trail-blazer, in that He took this road before us, and He is its perfecter (i.e., its perfect instance) in that He maintained confident hope of joyful resurrection and enthronement through shame and suffering greater than any that face His servants (2 ff., cf. 5.7–9). And as His example now inspires our faith, so His help and strength support it (2.18, 4.15 f.).

48 : The New Life-style

1 Peter 2.9–12; 4.3–6

Christians have a new *life* (2.9 f.). 'Called' by God from the 'darkness' of ungodliness into the 'light' of knowing Christ and salvation, they have 'received mercy' (wholly contrary to merit!) and become God's people. Now their task is that of priests, appearing before God to proclaim by praise and testimony what wonders He has done for them and can do for others. Peter echoes Exod. 19.5 f. and applies its thoughts to the Israel of the new exodus and the new covenant.

Christians must therefore have a new *life-style*, rooted in knowledge of two things. First, they do not belong in this world. Heaven is their home, and here they are only 'resident aliens' (persons without rights or legal status) and 'temporary dwellers' (11, cf. Heb. 11.13, where the thought is exactly the same). Their involvement in the world must therefore rest on, and be consistent with, clear-headed detachment from it. Second, self-indulgent and potentially vicious natural appetites are not the Christian's real self, whatever may have been true before conversion, and if given rein they ruin his spiritual health (11).

So with self-disciplined restraint Christians must say 'No!' to the ways of the world and the flesh, and stand apart from the wild company with which they previously identified (4.3 f.). Instead, they must maintain the practice of 'good works' (being good and doing good—'good conduct' [2.12 RSV] gets the idea). This will shame their critics—Christians always have critics —into recognition that God is in truth working in their lives, and so prepare the way for the critics' conversion (4.4; 2.12). Conversion, rather than the judgement of 4.5, 17 f., seems to be the 'visitation' in view here, for Peter is echoing Matt. 5.16 (on which see Study 45).

Chapter 4.6 is hard, but the least difficult interpretation understands it as clearing up a difficulty due to the fact that death is God's judgement on sin. Christians who have died will be shown at the judgement to be alive to God. On this point some early Christians, we know, were uncertain, cf. 1 Thess. 4.13 ff. Peter's purpose in v. 6 is then to ward off this uncertainty, lest his readers assume that the death of the 'dead' in v. 5 was proof that they were lost.

49 : On being Unsinkable
1 Peter 4.12–19

The word *suffering* covers a multitude of experiences, physical, mental and spiritual, from bereavement and a bad conscience to toothache and torture. Suffering in some form is every man's lot in this fallen and out-of-joint world (cf. Rom. 8.18–22), and the real 'problem of suffering' is the practical problem, how can we so handle it that it becomes a stepping-stone which takes us on rather than a stumbling-block which brings us down? Suffering enriches some and destroys others; the difference reflects what one brings to it. Christianity contains a secret which can make all suffering an enrichment, and this Peter discloses to Christians facing persecution (12).

Suffering Christians share Christ's sufferings (13). That is the secret! This can be said, not only of ill-treatment occasioned by our Christian profession (14, 16), but of all sufferings whatever (cf. Rom. 8.17), apart from legal punishment for crime or anti-social action, which Christians, Peter hopes, will not incur (15). As Jesus' experiences of temptation covered and transcended ours (cf. Heb. **2.**18; **4.**15), so with His experiences of frustration, pain, hardship, unfairness, cruelty, and the desolations of dying (cf. Heb. **5.**7 ff.); and as His sufferings in His own person led Him straight to glory, so will His sufferings in us lead us who are His (12; cf. **1.**6–11; Luke **24.**26; Rom. **8.**17). For both King and subjects, tribulation is the appointed road to the Kingdom; to be on that road authenticates one's Christianity (14), just as standing firm under pressure proves the quality of one's faith (12, cf. **1.**6 f.).

Suffering with Christ, then, is to be expected (12). Knowing what we do of its significance, we can rejoice in it (13: the verb is in the present tense, and means 'keep on rejoicing'). Recognizing it as a sign of blessing, we are to praise God, count it a privilege, and bear up, trusting our faithful Creator (14–16, 19).

Verses 17 f. introduce a sobering thought from a different angle. 'If God, the righteous Judge, so hates evil, and must deal with it, that He judges His redeemed people, what will be the fate of unbelievers, when His full wrath against sinners is revealed?' (A. M. Stibbs).

50 : Against the Devil

1 Peter 5.6–11; Ephesians 6.10–20

His Hebrew name (Satan) means 'adversary'; his Greek name (*diabolos*) means 'slanderer', 'evil speaker'. He is meaner, more cruel, and more destructive than anything we can imagine. He is a fallen angel kept for judgement (Jude 6); none the less, his present power warrants calling him ruler and god of this world (John **14.**30; 2 Cor. **4.**4). At the cross he was 'cast out' (John **12.**31), yet, though beaten, he is still fighting. His first enemy is God; he wants to thwart, spoil and bring to ruin everything God undertakes. So he fights Christians, because they are on God's side. Seeking to destroy God's work in their lives, he manipulates their circumstances and thoughts, so that their life becomes a series of 'temptations' aimed at their weak spots; and he never gives up. He is as fierce as a hungry lion (1 Pet. **5.**8), and utterly deceitful (Eph. **6.**11). Such is the biblical profile of 'your adversary the devil.'

What are we to do about him? Both Peter and Paul tell us to *resist* him (1 Pet. **5.**9; Eph. **6.**13, cf. Jas. **4.**7: the same Greek verb is used each time). Jesus' reaction when He detected that suggestions had come from Satan was to say 'No!'—'Get behind me, Satan' (Matt. **16**.23, cf. **4**.10)—and we must react the same way. Peter puts this point in the context of submitting to God (6), trusting His care (7), exercising self-control and being on guard (8), and standing firm in faith as troubles come (9). Paul builds up his famous picture of infantryman's armour given us by God to fit us for successful resistance—the belt, which is truth known; the breastplate, which is integrity followed; the shoes, namely readiness for action given by the gospel (or, perhaps, to serve the gospel); the shield, namely faith, by which Satan's 'fiery darts' (thoughts inducing despair) are deflected; the helmet, which is salvation known, the content of assurance; and the sword, which is God's message, His promise and command, which we must use against Satan as Jesus did in the wilderness (Matt. **4**.1 ff.). Prayer too, Paul adds, is vital (Eph. **6**.18).

We are to take Satan seriously, but not too seriously. For all his ferocity and cunning, Christ has conquered him, and we never need yield to him. Fight in God's way, say Peter and Paul, and God will see to it that you win (1 Pet. **5**.9 f.; Eph. **6**.11,13).

51 : This Way to Glory
Revelation 1.9–11; 2.8–11; 7.9–17

This world is the first of two which all men successively inhabit. The book of the Revelation, a product of persecution, written under the shadow of death (**1**.9 ff., **2**.10) and dealing with the Church's conflict between Christ's two comings—the war of the kingdoms of this world, we might say, with the Kingdom of God (cf. **1**.9; **11**.15; **12**.10)—maintains this two-world perspective throughout. Whether our experience of the second world will take the form of 'the second death' (**2**.11) or 'the crown of life' (**2**.10) is decided here on earth. Those who live 'in Jesus' (**1**.9, RSV), standing for the word of God (the gospel) and witnessing to Jesus, will enjoy what they have come most to desire with Jesus hereafter (**7**.15–17). Others will enjoy nothing hereafter (**20**.11–15); God's heaven would not be heaven to them, and in any case they will not be there. As in Revelation, so throughout the New Testament, these are the issues of eternity.

These passages depict the Christian's life on earth as *tribulation for Jesus.* 'Tribulation', meaning 'pressure', 'oppression', appears as the present experience of John (1.9), the immediate prospect for Smyrna (2.10), and the launching-pad of all the great multitude clothed in white (7.9, 14). As this company is probably the whole Church, so 'the great tribulation' (14) is more likely to be a generalized description of the whole gospel age than a limited reference to one particular climax of conflict (cf. 3.10). Satan and men on his string mount the tribulation (2.10), and by inflicting death seem to triumph; but theirs is not the last word.

For these passages also depict the Christian's life in heaven as *joy through Jesus.* Faithfulness maintained under pressure is true victory, and this is the conqueror's crown of reward (2.10 f.). Those in heaven are *completely cleansed* (Christ's red, shed blood washes their robes white—a glowing paradox) (7.14); they are *in God's presence always* (15, 'throne' and 'temple' signify a sense of God as present, potent, and adorable); they know *total contentment*, free from all that hurts (16); *Jesus cares for them constantly* (note, it is the Lamb, our sacrifice, who becomes our shepherd—another glowing paradox, 17, RSV); and *God turns all bitter memories into joy* (17b). Yes!—this will really happen.

John's radiant symbolism gives us, if not a literal preview, at least a faint flavour of 'the saints' everlasting rest', of which Richard Baxter sang:

> *My knowledge of that life is small,*
> *The eye of faith is dim;*
> *But it's enough that Christ knows all*
> *And I shall be with Him.*

Yes . . . exactly.

Questions and themes for study and discussion on Studies 44-51

1 List ways in which Christians ought to be different from the world around them.

2. How far is your church fulfilling Christ's command to be 'salt' and 'light'? What are the hindrances? How can they be overcome?

3. What biblical principles should guide the Christian when members of the family, parents and spouse, even, oppose his (or her) allegiance to Christ?

4. 'Laying aside every weight.' How much does 'weight' cover? How should one determine what falls under this heading?